H

Christ King Parish Library

D1130374

PRESENTED TO

CHRIST KING PARISH LIBRARY

by
Frank and Mary Bruce

PAUL VI

Critical Appraisals

Edited by JAMES F. ANDREWS

The Bruce Publishing Company / New York
Collier-Macmillan Limited / London

Christ King Parish Library

© Copyright, The Bruce Publishing Company, 1970

All rights reserved. No part of this book may be reproduced or transmitted in any form or by any means, electronic or mechanical, including photocopying, recording or by any information storage and retrieval system, without permission in writing from the Publisher.

Library of Congress Catalog Card Number: 78-131474

THE BRUCE PUBLISHING COMPANY, NEW YORK
COLLIER-MACMILLAN CANADA, LTD., TORONTO, ONTARIO

Made in the United States of America

Contents

Foreword

The genre of books exercising the critical function on living popes is almost nonexistent. As a result, the editor has had to create a methodology.

Two facts became immediately clear at the very beginning of the effort. First, the office of the papacy is so varied in its fields of responsibility that one man could hardly hope to do a serious critical work on Pope Paul and have it ready for publication during the pope's lifetime. And since the purpose of this book is to offer a living pope the kind of critical feedback that political figures enjoy and profit by, participation by more than one author was necessary in order to distribute the responsibility.

Secondly, it became clear that selectivity of areas to be addressed would be pivotal. The pope can be viewed from many angles. If we were to have a manageable book, the list must be winnowed ruthlessly.

The editor's controlling idea of the issues was determinative on both of these counts. The areas selected reflect his view of the papacy as the most significant international office capable of expressing moral values.

Therefore, this is not a "churchy" book. Rather, it is outgoing. The core of the book deals with Paul's leadership in these areas: the "oppressed consciousness" (youth, blacks, and Third World), peace and war, the worldwide desire for a share in decision-making power (collegiality), the key issues that Paul VI has had to meet within the church (birth control and celibacy), and his ability to unite men of religious concern (ecumenism). The book also contains two essays which view Paul's reign as a whole from differing stances. In addition, there are two essays included for background: the pope's biography and a chronology of his reign.

The editor is grateful to the men who have so generously responded to the invitation to participate in this critical venture. All of them have taken their responsibility seriously.

We are also grateful to the Bruce Publishing Company for having the courage and imagination to embark on this project.

No foreword could be complete without thanks to my patient wife, Kathleen, who created a climate to enable this work to go from idea to reality; and to my sons, Hugh and James, who provided the comic relief at just the right moments.

The Pope
in an Age of Insecurity

James F. Andrews

Mr. Andrews is executive vice-president and editor
of Universal Press Syndicate. Prior to his present
position, he was managing editor of the *National
Catholic Reporter,* managing editor of *Ave Maria,*
and an editor for Sheed & Ward.
His books include *The Citizen Christian* and
The Perplexed Catholic (coauthored with John
Reedy). He is also the editor of two volumes of
critical essays: one on the theology of Karl Barth,
entitled *Karl Barth;* the other entitled *Creative
Suffering: A Ripple of Hope.*

7

The office of the papacy has known many political and cultural landscapes. And its occupants have exhibited most of the catalogued variants of human personality.

When one reflects on the sharp dimensions of the papal landscapes and persons, he cannot escape being awed by the office's inner stability and flexibility. We can meld the two aspects of milieu and person in striking historical images; the hunted men of the papacy's first three centuries; Pope Melchiades with the beneficent stranglehold on Constantine; Leo courageously confronting Attila the Hun; Hildebrand bringing Henry IV to his knees; Urban II calling for the Crusades; the notorious profligate Alexander VI; Paul III and his Council of Trent; Pius X, the pastoral saint and heretic hunter; the beloved John XXIII, the transitional pope who became history's confounder.

The journey from the Catacombs to the Vatican City of today is an incredible one. The papacy has withstood tremendous challenges both from within and from without. Although it is true that power is invariably personal, as Adolf A. Berle states in his brilliant work, *Power,* it is also true that the office and the institution which sustains it overflows the person to whom the power is entrusted. The office of the papacy is well anchored in the community of the faithful—and beyond the community as well.

In a certain sense, then, the person who takes the long view could well afford to be sanguine about the odds in favor of the papacy's withstanding the contemporary storm. In fact, what is characterized today as turmoil and thunder in the Roman Catholic Church is of footnote proportions given the ruptures of the past.

This does not mean that the crises of today are insignificant. It simply means that if one grants certain presuppositions about the continuity of history, the occupant of the papacy—even if the office were reshaped according to the vision of the most utopian proponent of collegiality— would still be a person to be taken into serious account in the future.

The long view, what I would call the temptation to allow the office to overshadow the *person* holding power (the incumbent), is based on more than the assurance of history's beneficence to the papacy. This view springs from an emphasis on the transcendent basis of the papacy to the neglect of its incarnational reality.

As a result, this detached perspective, with its reliance on a continuing providence, retards the development of fresh imperatives on the power of the incumbent and places a psychological brake on the work of placing the pope within the context of his present responsibilities and options.

The church has itself run from the burdens of its ongoing incarnational role in every aspect of its life. As a result, we have seen fossilization confused with transcendence at various times (or ages) in its structures, its law, its sacraments, its concept of ministry—every aspect of its life.

In other words, Christ's promise to be with the church has often been inadequately interpreted, and, as a result, stunts rather than encourages the drive for perfection.

So it is always worth a man's effort to take a criti-

cal look at the papacy and its occupant. There is no inexora-
ble logic about the shape of the office and the exercise of its
power. History shows that the Spirit can adapt. And as Hans
Küng sharply pointed out to Karl Barth, the pope, though he
is the vicar of Christ, is only the *vicar* of Christ. The stakes
are high enough at any time in history to measure the performance of the occupant of Peter's chair against the ideals and
claims of the office. A quick inventory of the atrocities committed in the name of Christ by his vicars, or with their per-
missiveness, is a sure convincer of the value of the critical
function.

Popes have seldom enjoyed the immediacy of critical feedback available to other leaders. Even in this century
when communications facilitate such immediacy, popes have
been relatively immune. At best, papal feedback has been
spotty. A Roosevelt or a Churchill could count on his leadership receiving full critical evaluation; Pius XII could not, and,
in fact, he did not receive it. John XXIII was such a breathtak-
ing difference from Pius XII that even today it is impossible to
get sufficient distance to do anything but praise and to add the
conditional, now-common phrase: "But if he had lived after
the Council, he, too, would have found his leadership turning
sour. . . ."

Paul VI has been more fortunate. He has received
critical attention. However, most of this criticism has taken
place in the heat of journalism, and its full effect has been
easily discounted or deflected. What has been done in more du-
rable form has either read like hagiography or been blunted
by too much deference.

This book shares some of the weaknesses of journalism in its style. This style was not chosen by accident nor
completely by default of ability but, rather, in an attempt to
share in one of the strengths of journalism: immediacy. The
contributors are convinced that serious, critical attention is of
more value to a live pope than to his successor. Furthermore,
the questions raised here are urgent. They matter today, and

they are important because they are concerned with issues and the needs of people.

One avenue to taking Pope Paul's measure is to see if any glimpse of his own concept of the office emerges from the broad picture of his leadership to date. If we can grasp Paul's idea of the role of the pope, we might discover the basic criteria for our work.

Paul's reaction to the ferment or revolution occurring in the church has undergone deep changes in the past six years. His public statements reflect the depth of the psychological impact the postconciliar experience has had on him.

In his coronation address, Paul swept aside the pessimistic appraisals of modern man and confidently asserted that "it is easy to find the profound voices of this modern world, which is also stirred by the Spirit and by grace."

His grasp of the church's mission echoed the outgoing vigor of the Council: "We will continue to offer unremittingly to mankind today the remedy for its ills, the answers to its appeals."

At the end of the Council in 1965, he said the church in Council should be given credit for "our own new type of humanism: we, too, in fact, we more than many others, honor mankind." The vision of his pontificate as expressed in its earliest days was *ad extra:*—he was to be a pope concerned with peace, he was the traveling pope who would bring the gospel to all men. There was a buoyancy to him, a spontaneity that had not been foreseen at his election. The "Hamlet" characterization and the remark that "Since he was following Pope John, he could be excused in advance" were belied by his immediate resumption of Vatican II, by his bold announcement of a papal journey to the Holy Land, his announcement of the formation of the Synod of Bishops, and his intent to reform the Curia.

The main thrust of these early years therefore was marked by confidence in the church's new self-understanding, usually identified with Pope John and the Second Vatican

Council. That self-understanding included the church as a pilgrim people, the church with a mission of service to the world, the church as rejecting as outmoded and unevangelical its past stance of sole bearer of salvation and a guardian of truth which would condemn, anathematize. The church recognized its need for self-reform, for updating, for what was called *aggiornamento*.

The years of the Council were hopeful years. The world watched in amazement at the boldness of the pope as he asked forgiveness for the church's part in the breach during the Reformation, as the Council Fathers passed the document on religious liberty and made public conciliatory moves toward the Jews and other non-Christians. There was an irrepressible vitality that emanated from Rome.

What subsequently happened should have been expected. The Council Fathers thought that the vision they promulgated with the pope could be implemented at their pace. They were the architects; they would be the builders, too. In far too many cases they had not read the blueprints carefully enough before signing on the dotted line.

The pope himself did not take into account the politics of the situation. He would soon find himself isolated with the curial power structure that fought the Council and in their grasp, the grasp of the system, buttressed by a Roman subculture and the old stifling theological constructs.

The bishops, for their part, went back to their local churches and found that the Council documents had been read and taken seriously. One of the basic themes that sounded good on paper, the idea of the church as the People of God with all acting "coresponsibly," boomeranged. The Council Fathers found that although they had rightfully been architects, they had written into the blueprint the proviso that they would not be the sole overseer of the future building.

The Council was the genesis of a liberating theology. It was the locus of liberating acts. This set in motion the forces for a broad acceptance of the Council's mandate as serious and ready for implementation.

One rule of power that Paul did not take into account was that the acts of promulgating the conciliar decrees, which proclaimed a mandate to Christians throughout the world to take up a new vision of the church, was to have consequences which he could not control. Bishops throughout the world came to discover the same thing when they returned home after the Council.

In Paul's case, his act of breaking out of the prison of the Vatican, for example, to trace the steps of Jesus in the Holy Land, was symbolic to priests and other religious of their own need to shatter historic idiosyncratic conventions that governed their lives.

Adolf Berle states well what can result. Although he is speaking in a different context of power, his insight applies to what has happened in the church: "One impact of power-holding on the holder is his discovery that the power act, the direction of an event, causes surprisingly unpredictable consequences. What it signifies to the men affected—a matter determined by their emotions and minds—is ultimately more causative than the thing done. That causation cannot be controlled; certainly not by him. The power to cause an event has scant relation to capacity to control the feelings and opinions of men about the thing done, or assure their adhesion to a larger plan."

Reaction and retrenchment are the results we have seen in Paul. Fear and uncertainty. The same can be said of most bishops throughout the world when met with the same reality in their local areas.

Since then, Paul has been under heavy pressure to pull back. In view of the situation, he has maintained remarkable balance these past several years. But a trend toward pessimism, toward frustration and lack of hope has been clear. A random look at his statements since then shows him describ-

ing the church as under seige both from within and from
without. On November 23, 1966, he was talking about the
temptation "of believing that innovations derive from the doc-
trines and decrees of the Council give the go-ahead for any
kind of arbitrary change." In October of 1968, he pleaded for
a return to obedience. In March of 1969, he decried "giddi-
ness" among priests. In January 1969, he cried out: "How
many things, how many truths are questioned or doubted!
How many liberties are taken with the authentic patrimony of
Catholic teaching!"

In the days after *Humanae Vitae,* the concentration
on the church and on his authority has escalated. He has publicly verbalized his suffering several times and has even wept.
In a remarkable address on September 10, 1969, he admitted
that he had been reproached by a friend for appearing to be
guilty of "lack of confidence." He went on to assert his confidence, his hope. But then he reverted to a long discourse on
his suffering in the same talk:

"How could the Pope and those who bear the responsibility of giving the church pastoral guidance together
with him not suffer as they see *the major difficulties* are today
rising out of the church herself, that the *most poignant pain*
comes to her from the indocility and infidelity of certain of
her ministers and some of her consecrated souls, that the most
disappointing surprises come to her from circles that have
been the most assisted, the most favored and the most beloved?" (Emphasis added.)

He has called the situation a "crisis of faith," a "crisis of authority," a "crisis of obedience," among other things.

It is at least a crisis of identity.

Space does not permit us to document evolution of
the pope's and the church's full return to narcissistic concern. However, it is not too difficult for the reader who has
even been peripherally interested in the Catholic Church to see
that it has in the past several years reverted to largely an in-

tramural preoccupation, a housekeeping affair. The issues that have merited the full energy of the pope have been within his own chambers. The "new humanism" directing the church outward was clipped in early flight. The italicized phrases above are but slight evidences of the inversion that occurred. These are the "major difficulties, the most poignant pain!"

Finally, the identity crisis did find a sublimative target: the papacy itself and its exercise of authority. The papal critics linger on it; a full Synod of Bishops has just debated it; the International Theological Commission has a mandate to explore it. It has become the major theological problem facing the Catholic Church.

Ironically, the question of the manner of collegial exercise of the papacy barely squeezes by as a theological question at all. It is clearly a political question; unfortunately, the highest levels of the church cannot talk openly about politics—they *are* politicians instead. The political question involved is whether or not Paul will swing his power in such a way that the consultative sphere of influence of the papacy extends to all the world's bishops rather than just to the inhabitants of the Roman Curia and others who have Roman hearts but American or European skins.

From this broad picture, we can see that Paul considers the papacy chiefly as an office which has a primary duty to preserve the juridic, legal prerogatives of the office within the institutional church. It would not be simplistic to say that Paul, in fact, exercises the papacy as though its authority or power were determined, static—a measurable quantity—as though *legal* primacy is all he inherited on assuming the office. He shows little understanding that although he has had the office conferred upon him, it is up to him to assume the *power* of the office. Election carried no guarantee except the license to power. Popes have defaulted in the past. Their own concept of the papacy, their concept of the mandate, their understanding of the message and power of Christ, can limit or expand the amount of power they assume. If the office is viewed juridically rather than evangelically, the results can be a minimal claim on power.

Strange that in the eyes of critics the juridic approach to the papacy seems to amount to a maximalist claim. Paul, in most liberal quarters of the church, seems to be a maximalist. But the contrary is actually true. He is so fearful of dimunition of authority, so concerned about diluting the authority of the primacy of the office, that he is not assuming power. He is not a powerful pope because his vison of the office is circumscribed by the theological cultural and political constructions, such as Vatican I, which are hardly in touch with the rich power of the roots of the office: the evangelical mission.

It is interesting that the whole discussion today is over the question of authority; it is no accident that the active category of "power" is not used. Power is authority and yet authority is more suitable to legalistic concerns. Power is exercised. It is active. No one is particularly concerned about Paul's power.

In the long view of history, even one which put balance into the transcendentalist-incarnationalist temptations, Paul could emerge as a successful pope. The thinking might proceed in this way, all postconciliar periods bring unrest and aberrations. It is inevitable that anyone presiding over the church after such a revolutionary Council as the Second Vatican would find himself diverted from the primary goals of his reign.

Despite his diversion, Paul has taken steps that are historic: the improvement in Roman-Orthodox relations, his travels (especially the address before the United Nations), his dialogue with the Communists, his landmark encyclical *Populorum Progressio*. Currently, he is showing signs of perceiving that the drive to coresponsibility or collegiality is not a theological threat to his primacy but an attempt to strengthen his office by broadening the sources of consultation for papal decisions, and that it is really a political problem and can be solved.

All of this is true, and if we were to accept the concept of the papacy that Paul has, in the main, followed in his acts, we could accept the judgment that he is a successful pope. If, for example, we put him side by side with his chief mentor, Pope Pius XII, he towers. They both view the papacy in the same manner.

However, it is not only the pope's concept of the papacy that matters. He does not function as the sole source of criteria for measuring his leadership.

If we refuse to narrow the office to Paul's vision, if we insist on placing the papacy into an evangelical vision and juxtapose that vision with the opportunities and responsibilities of today, Paul can be seen as a pope who has failed to respond to the possibilities of his office—in serious, basic areas.

Time can be cruel. A man who might look good in one time can look impoverished in another. Unfortunately, man and his time have no choice but to live together.

In this writer's eyes, time has been especially cruel to Paul because it has offered him an unprecedented opportunity for power, and he has failed to grasp it. To understand the *moment*—his time—he would have had to shed the carefully instilled set of presuppositions his tutors taught him about the world and the church. To grasp the dimensions of the *power* he would have had to reach deeper into the roots of the papacy than his predecessors.

The world, society—whatever we want to call the locus of the Christian—has done an ungracious thing to men with a moral message. It has dared to shatter most of the neat legitimizers that men who represented moral values could use to shield themselves from the full force of their role. In one stroke, as John F. Kennedy said, the central questions facing man became moral questions. The groundwork of the shattering was laid with the conception of the Manhattan project. The new order began when conception became reality, when the mushrooms hid the shame and fury of man's most abominable acts at Hiroshima and Nagasaki.

Never before has history allowed itself to be marked so loudly; never before have the true dimensions of a new age been so slowly perceived. The year 1945 was more than a mark in history—the beginning of a new era in the saga of man, like the industrial age—it was a rupture in history; a discontinuity.

Although it seems that life goes on as before, although it seems that human consciousness is in normal continuity with its past, a new element has intruded. The threat of destruction by nuclear holocaust is real and ever-present. According to Karl Jaspers, it is *the fact* of human consciousness.

This fact has had tremendous implications for mankind. In addition to making all questions moral, it has ushered in a frantic age, an age that would blot out the basic insecurity of its consciousness by stockpiling security in every form and using every means possible to hide the reality from itself.

Dr. George Wald, Nobel prize winner in medicine and physiology in 1967 and professor of biology at Harvard University, made an extraordinary speech at the Massachusetts Institute of Technology on March 4, 1969, during a one-day "research halt." In this speech the septuagenarian attempted to describe what is bothering the youth of the world, especially American youth: the threat of total nuclear destruction.

He related the mega-murder-mathematics potential of the nuclear powers to show how callous we have become to gruesome statistics. After describing what the world would be like after reciprocal nuclear strikes by major powers ("Not a bang, and a certain number of corpses to bury, but . . . millions of helpless, maimed, tortured, and doomed survivors huddled with their families in shelters, with guns ready to fight off their neighbors, trying to get some uncontaminated food and water,"), he went on to pinpoint what is troubling youth:

"I think I know what is bothering the students. I

think that what we are up against is a generation that is *by no means sure that it has a future.*

"Are we to have a chance to live? We don't ask for prosperity, or security. Only for a reasonable chance to live, to work out our destiny in peace and decency. Not to go down in history as the apocalyptic generation."

It has taken over twenty years for the articulation of this consciousness to become as clear as it is today. And today, it is but a flicker of self-awareness. Even in the countries of the major nuclear powers, the people do not realize the life-destroying power that lies in their plains, in their fields hidden under silos. In the United States, for example, there is no general consciousness of the horror of what it means for 12 per cent of our gross national product to be spent on weaponry systems or what an 80-billion-dollar defense budget means.

Consciousness of an historical rupture of these dimensions takes time to permeate all levels. Pius XII did not grasp its meaning. John instinctively acted upon an understanding of it. Vatican II attests to the instinct. Paul, despite his pleas for peace, despite his noble efforts before the United Nations, his interventions on behalf of Vietnam and Biafra, has not evidenced a basic grasp of the meaning of the influence of the nuclear age on mankind and on the church's role.

There are basic indications of Paul's failure to appreciate the time in which he lives. To be fair, we must admit that consciousness needs time to understand. Time is needed for our actions to take on recognizable patterns, patterns which can point to a fundamental imbalance in the world's psyche. Pius XII went to his death not knowing that gas ovens had created a new moment for the papacy, much less knowing that the horror of what happened in Japan had thrust it into a new world.

The world's politicians were aware of the historical rupture to some degree. The rush to create and ratify the United Nations was not only because of the hatred of war; it was also the recognition that the newly unleashed power re-

quired supranational leadership and values, that survival ultimately would come from a supranational order.

If we take the papacy with utmost seriousness, and
accept its claim as supranational moral power, then we can
see that the United Nations and Vatican City have parallels.
The secretary general of the United Nations has, in fact, at
times filled in the moral vacuum provided by the papacy's
lack of initiative in world affairs. That office is the only one
which can claim to rival the possibilities of the papacy today.
And the fact that we could even think of comparing the two
shows to what extent we have accepted the circumscribed visions of the men who have held the office of pope.

The irony of the present struggle within the church,
then, is that the whole discussion of papal authority is taking
place when the office of the papacy has arrived at the moment
for which it was created. The message which it proclaims is
one of life and love—everlasting life. The founder of the office of the papacy himself legislated the norms for credibility
of a person's concern for eternal life, and they all involved
concern for present human life. In order to be credible when
proclaiming the message of eternal life, the messenger must
establish his concern for existing life. A world where life has
met its most formidable threat in history is a world ripe for
the message of life. An office based on the liberating force of
repentance, metanoia, change of heart, an office whose power
is precisely the power to change hearts, has its moment of
challenge.

If the pope sees his role as other than the proclaimer
of life, the liberating voice who has the power to change hearts,
if rather, he sees himself as a leader only in a juridic, legal,
defensive way, then he has failed to accept the weight of the
office. He has failed to take it seriously.

It is interesting to see that non-Christians view the
papacy in this way. Here is Rabbi Marc H. Tanenbaum's (of
the American Jewish Committee) assessment of Pius XII:
"I believe firmly that the Pope, *by his self-definition*

as the vicar of Christ on earth, had no moral alternative but to make his voice heard, clearly and decisively, in protest against the murderous evil of the Nazis. As Gordon Zahn, the Catholic sociologist, has demonstrated in his study, *German Catholics and Hitler's Wars,* the absence of clear-cut moral leadership on resistance to collaboration with Hitler's war machine and murder factories either from Rome or the German bishops at Fulda reinforced a mentality among German masses to conform to Nazi demands." (Emphasis added.)

Rabbi Tanenbaum's indictment of Pius XII shows how the historic evangelical claims of the papacy can haunt the incumbent.

It must be pointed out that Paul has evidenced appreciation for the evangelical role of the papacy at various points in his reign to date. In the coronation address already mentioned, he characterized as "superficial" the idea of modern man as a stranger to "all that is spiritual and religious." He saw modern man as aspiring for justice and peace. He went on to say, "For the sake of these causes, the world shows itself capable of practicing to a surprising degree the virtues of strength and of courage, the spirit of initiative, of dedication, of sacrifice. We say it without any hesitation: *All this is Ours.* And for proof We need only the immense ovation that everywhere greeted the voice of a pope (John) who recently invited men to organize society in brotherhood and peace (the encyclical *Pacem in Terris*) . . . Will Our voice be heard?" (Parenthetical remarks added.)

Note the phrase: "All this is Ours." A startling acceptance of world moral leadership. Note his optimistic characterization of modern man. And his proof of the papal role and power in the experience of John's reception.

It was only later that he was to dilute this commitment and to scorn modern man. Later, after he began to realize that the new role he had embraced was taking him and the church into unfamiliar waters, he spoke differently of modern man and the church's role.

We cannot hope here to document the entire range of opportunities passed by. We can only isolate *one* basic theme of Christ's teaching that has particular relevance to the contemporary situation and use this one theme as the evangelical criterion for Paul's leadership.

Fortunately, the contemporary world and Christ's message provide dramatic results when they are juxtaposed in the matter of security. It is possible for a person to argue that Paul has witnessed to Christ's gift of life, that he has taught decisively that man must respect human life if he is to be credible in his thirst for eternal life. (See *Humanae Vitae.*) However, the counterpoint must be present consistently in his leadership. How has he conveyed these moral values to the world? Is his message crushed by the reality of his actual life style? In other words, has he destroyed his credibility by the insecurity of his own leadership?

If life is the message, then insecurity is the media and the means. In other words, if life is to have a future on this planet, the world's citizens are of necessity to be led to a willingness to accept insecurity. If nuclear stockpiling is to cease, then insecurity must become a way of life. If food is to be shared with the nations that hunger, then insecurity must be part of the cost. If the exploited are to be liberated, the exploiter must loosen his grip, and thereby his security. If life is to be honored, if human life is to find a champion, the message must be one of insecurity to a world which has become frenzied in a search to be secure. If "peace is indeed to be progress," then there has to be a flesh and blood redistribution of insecurity.

A new order must come about if Paul's vision in *Progressio Populorum,* if Christ's vision in the gospel, are to become realities. To lead effectively in this time, a leader cannot view himself or his role from a stance that cannot imagine any other role or situation for himself—especially if he is offering the new vision for society.

But as recently as January 15, 1969, Pope Paul offered a different view of modern man, one which expressed the scorn that has become typical of him in recent years. "He is seized by a frenzy, he is exalted by a fury to overthrow everything (and here we have a worldwide protest) in blind belief that a new order (and this is an old world), a new world, a kind of rebirth not yet properly perceivable, is inevitably about to dawn." (Parenthetical remarks his.)

Instead of a new dawn, it may well instead be Armageddon because of a lack of moral leadership for the cause. The pope who once could understand these frenzied voices and could see that he had something to say to them now mocks their search for a new order. This is a significant matter when one considers that the pope is vicar of the man who proclaimed a new order, the man who thought the unthinkable and led men to preach what was, to put it mildly, a contradiction and a stumbling block. Such basic themes as Turn the other cheek, The first shall be last, Go an extra mile, Give him your cloak as well, Do not worry about tomorrow—all of these themes converge as a call to a willing acceptance of a life of insecurity for a new dawn.

Where are men to look today for such a call? Where are men to see such a life style? Is there any man or institution that has a liberated consciousness, that can see that technology, more consumer goods, and more stockpiling of weapons are all false securities?

Two examples suffice to show that Paul finds himself unable to willingly *live* the insecurity that the world is looking for.

In the area of theology, he has insisted countless times on the immutability of doctrinal formulations to the point that it is clear that he is obsessed with verbal security. Instead of seeing the message of the gospel as liberating, he sees it as a treasure to be guarded—and guarded in formulations that meet the needs of particular cultures. On August 9, 1967, he stated, "The definitions worked out by the Council must remain unchangeable in content and in the formulae that express it."

His "Credo for the People of God" is a concrete expression of this need for the security of formulations. In addition to the surface matter of verbal security, there is the deeper reality that the formulations support an understanding of the church that is preconciliar. In other words, Paul uses doctrinal purity as a polemic against the new mission of the church promulgated by Vatican II.

In the Credo, for example, Father Richard McBrien demonstrates how the involvement of the church in matters of political and social consequence are subtly undermined. The pope's Credo, says McBrien, assures "men that the Kingdom of God which we seek is in the next world, that insofar as it exists here and now it consists in the knowledge of Christ, hope of eternal blessings, an ardent response to the love of God, and the bestowal of grace and holiness among men."

Paul's frequent strictures against institutional change in the church need no documentation here. He has constantly flailed against structural change as well as change in the life style of religious. No proposed change *within* the church seems too minute to slip past the process of gradualism and caution that marks his style of leadership.

Another example, one particularly relevant since it is in an area where his leadership should be presumed to be confident, is that concerning priests. Speaking of priests in February of 1969, he said, "The priest feels like a strange social phenomenon—anachronistic, powerless, useless, even ridiculous. And then comes the new and dynamic idea. Something must be done. Everything must be dared to get near the people again, to understand them, to evangelize them."

But after seeing the problem and noting that experimental ministries are being formed, he bemoans the fate of those who want conventional priests and adds the very provocative self-portrait: "and all for the sake of adventures whose outcome is uncertain."

Note carefully the phrase "adventures whose outcome is uncertain." Recall that this is the pope who said that expropriation of property in under-developed countries is justified in *Populorum Progressio*. However, when he faces the

need for revolutionary change in forms of ministry, he balks
even at experimentation.

These few examples are sufficient to make the point
that although Paul is remarkably acute in perceiving the problems facing modern man, he cannot bring himself to accept
the risk of insecurity in the church itself. An age that is insis-
tently rushing toward its own destruction by a mad pursuit for
security has an unhappy, unwilling, and insecure pope.

As a result, his answers to the problems of our
times fall fatally short even when they are right. How can a
man who is so frightened of his own position that he is drag-
ging his feet on collegial action with his bishops expect a des-
pot to heed the pope's pleas on behalf of exploited people? For
freedom, for due process, for sharing in the decision-making
power? How can a man who refuses to make due process and
concern for basic human rights a reality *within* the church be
taken seriously by national leaders who can look at the Pope's
backyard?

How can the nations take a man seriously who asks
that ". . . even a small portion of national defense expendi-
tures be given to a world development fund . . ." when he justifies the wealth of art in the Vatican by rhetoric? For example, ". . . the grandiosity in external form which meets the
eye is not an empty show. It is all a solemn hymn whose deep
significance everyone may and should discover. Here is no expression of the senses, but of sensible beauty singing all the
glories of spiritual loveliness."

Politicians use rhetoric as well. They speak of nuclear weapons as the expression of a desire for peace, or as
necessary to insure a free world, or democracy, or human
well-being, etc. They justify economic exploitation in rhetoric
as convincing as Paul's.

If this pope is truly a vicar of Christ, if he is not
committed to security, then why is he so afraid to allow the
Spirit to work within the church? Why is he so afraid of new
theologies? Why is he so afraid of new approaches?

What if he took the risk of being a world moral

leader and made a fool of himself? Then there will be another pope. Popes live and popes die. Better to be a pope who risked for man's life and future than to be a pope who spent his years in the Vatican wringing his hands over doctrinal purity in a time when the world wants to see and hear and believe the Word—the liberating Word that breathes and lives and acts, not the Word that is captured in formulas in a purity that has the look of a whited sepulchre, pure and uninvolved.

The question still remains to be faced. If Paul did see his role to be broader and more demanding, what power does he have? What is this great Christian power that he can command?

We can but point to the influence of Pope John XXIII in so short a reign and the power he had of evoking the best from the world. He shared the apostolic awe of the greatest power in the world, the power to change a man's heart, to affect his life style by leading him to a new world view, a new way of looking at reality.

This power is the only power of the Christian. And it is not exclusively the Christian's. Other moral visions are competing for the hearts of men. Some are complementary to Christ's way; others are destructively opposed.

Power over a person's way of perceiving things is the power of religion. It can be used or unused; it exists.

That men of religion have such power and that it can be awesome can be testified to by the attempts of dictators like Joseph Stalin and Mao Tse-tung to cloak themselves with divinity. They seek not only physical dominion but the dominion that can come with priestly power.

Without entering into tedious preaching, two examples will suffice. Some years ago, there was a large biblical controversy over the interpretation of the miracle of the loaves and the fishes. Our social consciousness of the actual human situation was much more limited than it is today. Church leaders branded as heretical the view of some interpreters who were saying that actually Jesus had only touched the hearts of the multitude who were listening to him. His message caused them to open the lunches they had brought along and had been hiding because they didn't want to have to share with others. *This* was the miracle. Jesus had not literally multiplied loaves and fishes.

Today, when we look at this controversy in the context of papal power, which of these would be the greater miracle—if Jesus would come back today and multiply food and give it to the poor, the wretched and the hungry? or if he would change the hard hearts of that minute number of people who luxuriate in enough food for all?

Or, to make the point clearer in the context of our discussion, what is the greater power for the pope—to proclaim that he is infallible and for him to say something infallible? or for him to say or do something that would bring men to destroy their nuclear storehouses? Which is power? Which act is witness to the power and message of Jesus?

The pope is important in a global sense. Every Christian has Christ's power but it is the pope who can move an entire community by focusing it on the church's mission. It is only here that collegiality becomes a theological question, and it is here the pope has broken a basic law of power as defined by Berle: "Power must be delegated in order to be extended, and each fragment of power—handed downward through any organization—must yield a dividend of increased power to the central authority. When it does not, the central power holder must meet the issue or suffer."

Paul must meet the issue or suffer.

In our mind, then, the world is waiting for Christ's message. The church could make a decisive difference in the struggle for life. But the church needs confident leadership that can live the message of insecurity and allow it to undergo the risks necessary to shape itself for its task to the world. Or, to paraphrase Jesus Christ's words: "There is no profit in a church that gains order in its ranks and suffers the loss of its soul in the face of its historic mission."

The Anguish
of the Pope

Salvatore J. Adamo

Monsignor Adamo is a priest of the diocese of
Camden, New Jersey, and pastor of Immaculate
Conception Cathedral.
In addition to his pastoral work, he is the
controversial editor of the *Camden Star-Herald*
and contributes a regular column on the press
to *America* magazine. He is author of a book
entitled *While the Winds Blew,* and is a
frequent guest on radio programs in the
Philadelphia area.

It may be an apocryphal anecdote, but if so it pinpoints the posture of the present pontiff more precisely than any true story. It happened shortly after the storm of reaction erupted over the issuance of Paul VI's world-letter *Humanae Vitae*. Talking one day to a group of pilgrims, the Pope suddenly cried out, "Look into my eyes and tell me if I look to you like a reactionary pope. The Pope is not a reactionary pope or a progressive pope. He is the Pope and that is all."

That is why the pope is contradicted on all sides —he won't take sides. He prefers to guide gently and plead persistently with first one group then the other. He is determined not to widen the polarization of the church. He yearns to heal divisions and unify all people who bear the name of Christian.

So far he is succeeding, although somewhat tenuously. Despite anger and resentment leveled at him to a degree no pope has had to endure since the Reformation, he has managed to keep the church in one piece. Not in tranquil peace, but in one undivided piece. In achieving that much at least he is of one mind with Christ who had prayed ardently for the unity of his followers at the Last Supper.

The problem in understanding Paul VI's agonizing role is complicated by those Catholic intellectuals who have made pope-watching (and at times pope-baiting) a favorite post-Vatican-II sport. Almost from the start, every move Paul VI made, every utterance he pronounced was subjected to microscopic examination. Even his personality was compared unfavorably with Papa Roncalli's warm "world's father-figure." Forgotten was the fact that he had been John XXIII's choice, evidenced by John in many subtle ways, to succeed him. In fact, progressive Catholics were delighted when Paul VI ascended the papal throne. They looked to him to continue the *aggiornamento* and to crown it with the success death had denied to his great predecessor.

They believed correctly that as Cardinal Montini the new pontiff had pledged himself to do just that. Had he not said shortly before the Consistory in June of 1963, "John has shown us some paths which it will be wise to follow. Can we turn away from these paths so masterfully traced? It seems to me we cannot."

There was also the matter of his record in Milan, a record that stamped him as an outstanding pastoral-minded bishop, formed in the spirit of Vatican II. Here was a bishop who had sold church land to build chapels for the poor in outlying districts. And at the same time he had purchased small cars for the priests who would serve them. Moreover, he had recruited Neapolitan priests to care for the Southern Italians who had migrated north to earn bread by working in the booming factories there. He had provided housing and other assistance for the poor. Despite his aristocratic appearance, despite his long years in the Curia, he soon had become known as "archbishop of the workers."

It has been observed that, had he been elected pope after Pius XII, he would have dazzled the Catholic world with his progressive spirit. Coming when he did, he was overshadowed by the fabulous figure of John. In a way, it was like Truman following Roosevelt or Johnson after Kennedy.

In each case, their particular achievements were dwarfed by the monumental works of the charismatic leaders who preceded them.

In all fairness, then, let's look at the record, as Al Smith used to say. In doing so, we may discover that Paul VI is highly underrated.

Not only has Paul been overwhelmed by John XXIII but he has also in a sense been undermined by his former close association with Pius XII. For about the time that he became pope, an attack was launched against Pius, his great idol in the papacy, the man he had served so unsparingly. Had not Rolf Hochhuth in his play *The Deputy* portrayed the ascetical and aristocratic Pius XII as a cowardly, avaricious, effeminate anti-Semite? Had not many Catholic intellectuals believed the slander or a substantial portion of it? And had not the then Monsignor Giovanni Battista Montini been in the key congregation, the Secretariat of State at that time? Therefore, as a close collaborator of Pius XII, he became suspect too. The rumored sins of the father were visited on the son.

Nor was this distrust dissipated when the third and fourth sessions, now under his control, failed to produce the long-awaited declaration on the Jews. That declaration together with one on religious liberty "had become touchstones by which the progressives' progress was to be judged," as John Cogley had put it so neatly. Strangely, though, after both declarations were formally accepted at the final session of Vatican II, the distrust of Paul VI lingered on.

More strangely, this distrust was not even countered effectively by the fact that his first pilgrimage outside Rome had been to the Holy Land. His first greeting to modern Israel, "Shalom!" had been swallowed up by his loyal defense of Pius XII. Possibly it was undiplomatic to mention the man whose character Hochhuth had assassinated. But Paul VI was ever loyal, which may be why he prizes loyalty so highly himself. Nor was his loyalty a blind impulse. He knew that a

calmer review of Pius's relations to the Jews during the holocaust would vindicate the contention that no religious or political organization in the world did more at greater risk to save
Jewish lives than the Vatican with its relentless rescue operations.

Clearly, from the beginning Paul VI had many
handicaps to overcome. As time went on, these handicaps
were aggravated by an impossible philosophy or theology or
sociology of the papacy. On the one hand, papal infallibility
was challenged and its overreach deplored. On the other
hand, a practical infallibility was expected from Pope Paul
VI, who was allowed to make no errors, but rather exercise
instant and continuous infallibility. Whenever he stumbled, ever
so slightly, he was jeered at. Whenever he walked upright, ever
so magnificently, he was damned with faint praise.

That seemed to summarize the attitude of many
avant-garde Catholic writers who pontificated in a growing
number of Catholic and secular periodicals. That attitude is
most evident in Daniel Callahan's famous essay in the October 9, 1968, issue of the *National Catholic Reporter,* which
bore the title, "How to Get the Papal Monkey off the Catholic
Back." Somehow the article failed to portray Cardinal Ottaviani as the garlicky organ-grinder of its imaginative invention.
One passage epitomized the new ambivalent attitude toward
the papacy.

"I fail to see," said Callahan, "why the birth-control
encyclical should not be counted as infallible, if anything is to
be infallible. It was addressed to the whole church, it was *ex
cathedra,* it was solemn, and it concerned morals. It met all
the criteria established by Vatican I. That the encyclical is not
considered infallible, however, only gives a further indication
how far the theologians, the bishops and the papacy have
gone in insuring that papal infallibility should remain what it
is essentially, a vacuous doctrine."

Earlier in the same essay, he had written this about
the doctrine of papal infallibility: "It is proclaimed but un-

used, praised but untouched by human hands, which can find nothing to touch."

What Callahan seemed to be saying is that papal infallibility is no good unless it is used regularly. But then it should *never* be used because there's nothing there to be used. Or, to employ his own metaphor, no one should worry about the papal monkey on the Catholic back because it's only a figment of the imagination, anyway.

Such views were echoed and reechoed in America and many other lands since Vatican II ended. What has resulted is a widespread ignoring of the avowed goal of Vatican II, a goal that was expressed so lovingly by John XXIII in 1959: "By God's grace, then, we shall hold this Council; we shall prepare for it by working hard at whatever on the Catholic side most needs to be healed and strengthened according to the teaching of our Lord. When we have carried out this strenuous task . . . then we shall point to the church in all her splendor and say to all those who are separated from us, Orthodox, Protestants, and the rest, 'Look, brothers, this is the Church of Christ . . . Come, here the way lies open for meeting and for homecoming; come, take or resume that place which is yours, which for many of you was your father's place.' "

Such an avowed aim should be the criterion in judging the accomplishments of Paul VI as we stand on the threshold of the seventies. We must ask ourselves whether or not the pope has promoted reform in the church and advanced reunion with our separated brethren. On both counts I believe his record is admirable, and it is scarcely seven years since his pontificate began.

Consider his bold plan to reform and transform the Curia, that *bête noir* of progressive Catholics. He announced his intentions in a speech before the Council fathers on November 18, 1965. "The studies undertaken with a view to the reform of the Roman Curia have been advanced and have made good progress," reported the pope.

"We can say at once that apart from the replacement of personnel, there is no great necessity for structural changes. On the other hand, there is need for not a few reforms, for some simplifications and other improvements. The criteria that should animate this body will be determined and formulated with greater clarity. The desired transformation will be slow and partial but it cannot be otherwise if due respect is to be had for persons and traditions. But come this transformation surely will."

In testimony to his sincerity, on the day before the Council officially closed, the pope announced the reform and renaming of the dreaded Holy Office. Thereafter it would be known as the Congregation for the Doctrine of the Faith. Among the new rules under which it would operate was one that forbade the Congregation to denounce any book except "after hearing the author and giving him the opportunity of defending himself." Admittedly, the new change did not prevent all the old abuses, even after Cardinal Seper had replaced Cardinal Ottaviani. But the abuses were cut down and eventually may be eliminated entirely. Thoroughgoing reform simply requires time in institutions as well as among men.

It is also a matter of record that from 1966 through 1969 Paul VI made much progress in internationalizing the Curia as part of its reform. As an addenda to such weighty changes, much of the medieval pomp and circumstance surrounding Vatican ceremonies has been curtailed. Many royal titles have been abolished; even the prestigious monsignorship has been diluted, and hopefully will soon be suppressed. Undeniably, these are but halfway measures toward a return to greater simplicity in the church, a simplicity more in keeping with the spirit of Christ. But progress does proceed a step at a time; only revolution takes great leaps forward. Sometimes revolution wrecks more than it reforms.

Probably the most significant reform accomplished

by Paul VI was the establishment of the world Synod of Bishops. Although this body had been recommended by Vatican II, a pope lukewarm toward the *aggiornamento* could have ignored the proposal indefinitely. Had he been jealous of papal power, he would not have convoked the episcopal Synod in 1967 and again in 1969. True, little progress ensued from the 1967 gathering, much like the first session of Vatican II. But the second meeting of the Synod in 1969 proved to be an unexpected success. That arch-critic of the Vatican, the man who probably played an important role in Xavier Rynne's reports on Vatican II, Father Francis X. Murphy, had this to say about the 1969 Synod: "Pope Paul brought the extraordinary Synod of Bishops to an auspicious close October 27 with a talk that should make history.

"Brief, cheerful, and to the point, the Holy Father told the prelates he was in complete agreement with their recommendations. He would, in short order, put them into effect.

"The Pope likewise agreed that a special commission of prelates representing the episcopal conferences should be created. It will be attached to the office of the general secretary for the Synod in Rome.

"It will be this group's task to see that what the previous Synod decided is put into practice. It is to work out the agenda for the next Synod on the basis of recommendations sent to Rome by the diocesan bishops. Finally, its members are to serve as go-betweens for the curial officials as well as for the pope with the episcopal conferences in the exchange of information on important matters."

Murphy's concluding comment about the Synod was that "it seemed to indicate the Catholic Church has no intention of being discouraged, much less overcome, by its present adversities."

Paul VI therefore has not wrought merely minor changes in the Catholic Church. The trouble is that too many have allowed the vociferous dissent over his world-letters on celibacy and birth control to blind them to his many meaningful successes. Nor am I sure that generations to come will not bless him for maintaining the traditional teachings and discipline in those areas. It is not beyond the realm of possibility that the pope is right, even without having invoked his infallible teaching authority, elusive though it be.

Apart from his reform of the church, Paul VI has embarked on the greatest ecumenical adventures of any pope in history. Even before the Council ended, his pilgrimage to Jerusalem was climaxed by a moving meeting with Patriarch Athenagoras of the Orthodox Church. He and the patriarch prayed together for the unity of all Christians everywhere. Concerning the encounter, the patriarch said, "This is what we have awaited for centuries."

Nor was it a one-shot affair. Over the next five years, continuing contacts and dialogue kept clearing the road toward the reunion of Constantinople and Rome.

Other meetings followed with the heads of Protestant Churches including the Archbishop of Canterbury and American Protestant leaders like Bishop Fred Pierce Corson and Dr. Eugene C. Blake. These encounters were climaxed by the pope's visit to the World Council of Churches in Geneva late in June of 1969.

How effective have been the ecumenical efforts of Paul VI? In my opinion, they have surpassed the most optimistic hopes, even though much remains to be done. Recall, however, the proposal early in 1968 of Bishop C. Kilner Myers of the Episcopal diocese of California. Noting that the Lambeth Conference as well as the World Council of Churches were meeting that summer he said, "I propose that the leadership of these two conferences reschedule these events to meet together at Rome with the Pontiff and the bishops of the Roman Catholic Church. I propose then that the Roman pontiff be declared first among equals of the Christian Church on earth and that he establish a College of Christians, clerical and lay, to develop a base of Christian power that the national communities will heed."

Yet, it has been in his reaching out to the world that Paul VI has distinguished himself most. No other pontiff ever raised his voice more often or more passionately for peace. No other pontiff ever journeyed abroad to match words with deeds as he has. In short, he has become the world's best peace pilgrim.

His work for peace reached its peak during his visit to the United Nations on October 4, 1965. Not that his efforts abated after that, but his dramatic appearance before the United Nations General Assembly was the highlight of his continuing efforts for peace in Vietnam, peace in Nigeria, peace in the Near East, peace wherever war is raging.

"Many words," he observed before the United Nations, "are not needed to proclaim the loftiest aim of your institution. It suffices to remember that the blood of millions of men, that numberless and unheard-of sufferings, useless slaughter and frightful ruin, are the sanction of the pact which unites you, with an oath which must change the future history of the world: No more war, war never again! Peace, it is peace which must guide the destinies of peoples and of all mankind."

Then he added this tribute to the United Nations: "Gentlemen, you have performed and you continue to perform a great work; the education of mankind in the ways of peace. The United Nations is the great school where that education is imparted."

Some two years later, realizing that world poverty constituted one of the greatest threats to peace, he issued his historic world-letter "On the Development of Peoples." Whereupon, he called for world war on poverty. As he put it, "To wage war on misery and to struggle against injustice is to promote, along with improved conditions, the human and spiritual progress of all men, and therefore the common good of humanity. Peace cannot be limited to a mere absence of war, the result of an ever precarious balance of forces. No, peace is something that is built up day after day, in the pursuit of an order intended by God, which implies a more perfect form of justice among men."

In urging social reform, Paul VI spurned violence. However, reluctantly, he did admit its value as a last resort.

"We know," he said, "that a revolutionary uprising, save where there is manifest, long-standing tyranny which would do great damage to fundamental personal rights and dangerous harm to the common good of the country, produces new injustices, throws more elements out of balance and brings on new disasters." Two of the greatest social reformers of our day, Gandhi and Martin Luther King, Jr., would not have rejected this position of the pope, unless to insist perhaps that no conditions warranted "a revolutionary uprising."

Paul VI's attitude on racism, the third great disease of our age, needs no recording. His deeds outshine any words. His visit to Nigeria in 1969 and offer to remain there as long as necessary to help bring peace to a nation wracked by civil war, showed his deep love for the black man. Black bishops have been made in increasing numbers. Cardinals from every race, more than ever before, now stand at the pinnacle of the church's hierarchy. This unique lesson in brotherhood has not been lost on our generation.

In conclusion, I must point out that I have only touched briefly on the achievements of Paul VI, a pope whom history will honor despite his being grossly misunderstood and underestimated by so many Catholics of our day. Indeed, it is almost tragic to realize that Paul has been attacked mercilessly by many who should know better. As a result he has borne the anguish of lashings by those who feel he is too conservative and whippings by those who insist he is too liberal. Extremists of the right and left in the church have urged him to resign. But look at the record, even in brief outline. Have his accomplishments been so paltry as to deserve such contempt?

His only fault, if fault it be, is rooted in his ambition to fulfill what he described as his role. "The Pope is not a reactionary pope or a progressive pope," he insisted. "He is the Pope and that is all."

The Case Against the New Roman Catholic Spirituality

Rubem A. Alves

Dr. Alves, a native Brazilian, is a Protestant
theologian and author of the book *A Theology of
Human Hope.* He is currently preparing a study
on Third World theology for SODEPAX
(Provisional Committee on Society, Development,
and Peace of the Vatican and the World Council
of Churches).

Harvey Cox has described Dr. Alves as follows:
"The 'Third World'—the world of enforced
poverty, hunger, powerlessness, and growing
rage—has found a ringing theological voice in
Rubem Alves of Brazil."

The scope of an article dealing with the relationship of Pope Paul's leadership to the oppressed men of the world is indeed awesome. The options available for such a critique are disturbingly varied. One could look at his record of leadership among peoples of the Third World. Or one could isolate his performance toward the oppressed blacks or other similarly exploited minorities of men. Or one could look at the alienated youth of the world, for example, those of the Western democracies like the United States or France.

Blacks, the members of the Third World, and alienated youth may seem a strange combination at first glance. But when one reflects on the fact that even a well-fed man can have an enslaved or oppressed consciousness in a technological society—the fact that he has been made a passive consumer with constant encroachment on his ability to be creator of his own world—then it becomes clear that oppression can cross lines of poverty and wealth as well as of color.

In other words, rather than isolating a particular oppressed people, we shall deal in this article with the emerging consciousness of a world proletariat that is seeking—is groaning—for freedom.

To do this adequately, we must undertake what may appear to some as tedious analysis of the difference between an oppressed and free consciousness for a human being; we must discover an analytical framework for *interpreting* what a leader like Paul *says*. To provide this analytical framework, we must delve into the classic indictment of religion as functioning as an oppressor rather than a liberating force in society. We must look at the contemporary Roman Catholic theological message (I prefer the term "spirituality") to see if it has a message for the oppressed. And most important of all, we must look at Pope Paul himself to determine whether he is a liberating leader of this movement, or a horrified spectator attempting to stifle it.

The framework for analysis is essential if we are to avoid the pitfall of mistaking rhetoric for reality. Words are said in a context of a man's world-view, a set of usually unexpressed attitudes and presumptions about life and the world. A casual glance at the rhetoric of leaders and their use of words like "freedom," "peace," "rights," etc., especially while they are involved in oppressive actions like war or economic exploitation, clearly justifies the need to look below the surface of words in order to discover what is actually meant.

When Marx accused religion of being the opiate of the people, he simply pointed out what seemed to be an obvious social fact: that the real contradictions, injustices, and pains of the world were taken up by religion and solved magically in the world of the beyond. The human being whose consciousness was under the spell of religion and its language, although he felt the contradictions of the social conditions in which he lived, was made incapable of realizing the requirements for abolishing these conditions by the simple fact that for religion this task was God's and not man's business.

Religion thus functioned in such a way that the consciousness under its bewitchment could never take on the role of creator of a new world. It was reduced to a passive role, determined by the existing social structures, but never free to transform them.

Religious consciousness would thus be the same as oppressed consciousness, the consciousness of the slave who is never lord of his own future, since he belongs to someone else.

Religion, therefore, functioned as the ideology of the status quo, since it made it impossible for man to project his own liberation, and it maintained the power of those who oppressed him. To the extent to which religious ideals and hopes—which, in many senses, expressed man's dissatisfaction with the prevailing conditions of his world—remained restricted to the realm *beyond* history, these ideals were not only impotent to challenge the status quo but, more than that, they contributed to the perpetuation of things as they were. Religion maintained a repressed consciousness in a repressive world.

Was Marx right? It is beyond doubt that in the great majority of cases religion has functioned as the ideology which maintained the status quo. But is this the fate of religion? It is not possible for a religious ideology to become just the opposite, a utopia?[1] By a utopian religion, I mean a constellation of symbols which, as they are transformed in action, tend to break the status quo open for new possibilities?

The new Roman Catholic spirituality and the practical form which it has taken in a significant number of instances suggest compellingly that maybe we are witnessing the crucial event of the death of an ideological form of religion and, at the same time, its resurrection as a utopian spirituality.

One has simply to read the documents which express the concerns, hopes and commitments of those who are deeply involved in the front lines where the battles against the status quo are being fought to see that there is something new here.

[1] For a detailed discussion of ideology and utopia see Karl Mannheim, "The Utopian Mentality" in *Ideology and Utopia,* trans. Louis Wirth and Edward Shils (New York: Harcourt, Brace & World, Inc., 1936).

But, as we all know, statements can be deceptive if taken in themselves. This is why these documents must be read merely as footnotes to a *new style of life*—a new style of life that is so deeply committed to the transformation of the world that it has led many to martyrdom. It seems to me that it is beyond any doubt that the new Roman Catholic spirituality, still being formed, far from being the opiate of the people, is rather a beautiful example of how faith can destroy the oppressed consciousness of a man and transform it into one which is free to create the conditions for the liberation of the world.

Now, it is a fact that the transition from the oppressed consciousness to the free consciousness is not a natural result of the normal process of growth. "Unfreedom" does not become freedom just by becoming "mature." The transition from the one to the other implies a break, a leap, a rupture. Thus, this transition cannot be described in terms of evolution but rather as revolution.

I mention this simply to indicate that the process of liberation of the oppressed consciousness is one whereby it is restructured and reorganized. The goal of the process is not "maturity" but rather "a new being." This is what is implied in the New Testament word used to describe what is involved in conversion, *metanoia*. *But* when the new being comes into being the old one passes away. The old must die if the new is to be born: death and resurrection.

These remarks help us to understand what is happening in the Roman Catholic Church. Just as there is no smooth transition from the oppressed to the free consciousness, religion as an ideology which functions as an oppressing agent likewise does not *grow* into religion as an instrument for human liberation.

The new Catholic "utopian" spirituality is quite conscious of this fact. It knows that its liberating power is dependent on its freedom from religion as ideology. Religion as ideology and religion as utopia cannot exist side by side. It would be a gross mistake to believe it is possible to simply outfit the ideological structure of religion with utopian themes. This would be the same as putting new patches on old clothes.

Yvonne Lubbock expressed beautifully what we are trying to say. "One thing is sure," she says, "the old orthodox Catholicism which we once knew is dead. It is impossible to foretell the form under which it will be resurrected; but every conscious Christian will live by hope during the period of transition." [2]

So, the Roman Catholic Church, like a woman in travail, is giving birth to a new spirituality, bearer of a free consciousness. But our purpose goes beyond this point. We have to discover whether the newborn child is welcomed or not by the mother. To what extent was religion as "utopia" a consciously planned pregnancy?

To what extent is the magisterium of the church, represented by Pope Paul, in love with this new type of spirituality?

To what extent does an ideological structure of religion lurk under the overt articulation of utopian themes in official documents and statements? In order to answer such intriguing questions, we need first to examine the problem of the "free" and of the "oppressed" human consciousness from a closer distance.

Peter Berger, in his *Invitation to Sociology,* has a delightful chapter in which he shows that what we call the unity or continuity of our self is really a series of different biographies which we construct.[3]

---

[2] Yvonne Lubbock, "Acreditar e Ser," in Michael de la Bedoyere, *O Futuro do Christianismo Catolico* (Rio de Janeiro: Editora Paa e Terra, 1969), p. 39. Portuguese translation from the English original *The Future of Catholic Christianity* (Philadelphia, Pa.: J. B. Lippincott Co., 1966). Since the original is not available to this writer, the text is a translation of the Portuguese text.

[3] Peter Berger, *Invitation to Sociology* (Garden City, New York: Doubleday Company, 1963), pp. 54–65.

As we live, we are involved in a continuous process of "rewriting" our own history, and very often from radically different and even opposed angles.

This is so because we never look at our past objectively, as if it were a thing. We think always from the standpoint of our present emotions, values and commitments which could be properly called our "ultimate concern." I ask the reader not to endow this expression with the theological meaning which Paul Tillich gives to it. I simply want to indicate that human life is organized around, and structured by, the existential values to which a man is committed.

Our past (which could be seen as a simple chronological sequence of events which can no longer be changed) is thus taken up, organized, and valued according to *this* emotional center. It is now organized in zones of clarity and shadow, of shame and pride.

If we go, by any chance, through a vital experience which changes our values, our whole past is reorganized also. Very often light and shadow, pride and shame shift positions. The "I" is no longer the same. He still says "I," but he knows that his whole structure has undergone a structural revolution.

Memory, therefore, is not something fixed. It is organized, disorganized, and reorganized in a process of permanent interpretation and reinterpretation which is governed by the prevailing emotional center of our existence.

History is thus to some extent autobiography, because history exists only when we remember. And we remember always from the center of our existence. That which we call objective history, although it wants to be objective, contains always the *perspective* of the one who writes it.

This process is true not only for individuals but for groups. The past which a group preserves and remembers is always *their* past, that is, a past which is preserved in and organized by a memory which, in its turn, is governed by the concrete conditions of the existence of the group. Mannheim remarks that the purposes and hopes of a group are the organizing principles whereby it orders not only the future happenings but the past as well.[4]

The memories of a group contain the secret of its "soul"—what it loves and hates, what it fears and hopes. This is why history cannot be written once and for all. There are no "definitive" works. It has to be written over and over again by each new generation.

This is what separates man from the animals. Animals have, as men do, a history. They are the product of a long struggle for survival and the result of endless experiments aimed at creating better conditions for life. But animals, differently from men, do not remember this process.

The wisdom which was learned by the struggle for survival in time remains now stored in the body of the animal. Memory is preserved as organism. History becomes structure.

The animal, therefore, is held by its past and is never free in relation to it. This is why it cannot reorganize its memory, which means that it cannot reorganize itself! The animal is ready, finished, closed to the world, as its world is closed to him. It is its biological memory which "programs" how its world is organized and what it can do and has to do in order to survive.

With man the situation is different. His biological "program" is defective. He is not held captive by the past. He is free over it. It is *his present* which determines how he reads the past and *not* his past which determines his life in the present. The past becomes intelligible when it is assimilated by man's present experiences. Otherwise, it remains as something alien "out there" and is forgotten.

We are suggesting here a hermeneutical structure: a model for our interpretation of the past and of the future. We believe that we are very close to the biblical way of understanding time. The prophets looked at the past always in order

---

[4] Karl Mannheim, *op. cit.*

to see better the way to the future. The past has no right of its own. It is no longer alive. Memories only preserve images of former life. The past is remembered not for the sake of itself, as with the platonic anamnesis, but because it provides a clue, and nothing more than a clue, for us to discern the signs of the present and future. Only as architects of the future can we understand the past, remarked Nietzsche.

When is the consciousness of men oppressed or free? This question can be answered through other questions. Who is the master? Who is the servant?

Does man hold the past or does the past hold man? The oppressed consciousness is kept captive by the past. The past is its law. The past does not free but binds. It is not a horizon which opens towards the future but instead it is reified, ontologized.

Nietzsche's furious attack against Christianity and Western civilization was, to a large degree, based on his discovery that they had eternalized the past values, transforming them into metaphysics. And he believed that, as such, they had been forced upon man as the only possible models for the future. According to Nietzsche, God and religion were the powers which condemned man to an eternal neurosis: man's fate was to live in an obsessive repetition of the past. Man had become a crab; he walked backwards and thought backwards. History could not move towards the future.

For these reasons, Nietzsche believed it necessary to break the old values and to announce the death of the guardian of the past: God. When the past is the master over man, man becomes like an animal; he is not free over his "program." He gains an "essence" by becoming stabilized and loses his power to transcend himself.

However, the free consciousness is determined fundamentally by its freedom for the future. This is its ultimate concern, the existential center where it thinks and acts. Its freedom for the future transforms the past from law into grace. The past no longer defines the world. It is now apprehended as a tool for men to build new worlds. The issue is never whether or not we take the past seriously. There is no such option.

The real problem is: Who is the master? Man or the past? Who uses the other? Man or the past? Who is the "definer?" Does the past "define" man's history or is man free to rewrite his own biography, thereby resurrecting his own past under new forms?

But the past does not exert its power only through our memories. Kolakowski, in his essay *The Priest and the Jester,* gives the name of "priesthood" (for obvious reasons) to one type of consciousness which is under the bewitchment of the past.

And he adds the following remark: [5] "Priesthood is not merely the cult of the past as seen through contemporary eyes, but the survival of the past in unchanged shape. It is thus not only a certain intellectual attitude towards the world, but, indeed, a form of the world's existence, namely, a factual continuation of a reality which no longer exists."

Through the preservation of the past, the dead exert their power over the living ones!

Nietzsche was the prophet. Today we live his prophecies. Man set out to rewrite his biography, to liberate himself both from the intellectual bewitchment of the past and from its politico-institutional grip. As the oppressed consciousness dies, a new one comes into being. You can call this man the one who is no longer under tutelage, as Kant and Bonhoeffer did. (Or call him the secular man, the protester, the one who breaks old values. Names are important only to the extent to which they are footnotes to life.)

What is important to see is that the universal groaning (Rom. VIII:22) which we hear today in the mouths of protesters, iconoclasts, revolutionaries and heretics (names

[5] L. Kolakowski, "The Priest and the Jester" in Maria Kuncewicz, ed., *The Modern Polish Mind* (New York: Grosset & Dunlap, 1963), p. 326.

which are used by those who want to preserve the present) is the dark side of a joyful discovery that man can be free, that a new future can be created. The common denominator of protest is the discovery that the future does not need to be the simple expansion of the past, that history is not like an orgnism which grows without interruptions. Man can be the creator, "the subject" of history and the master of his own future.

The same universal groaning for freedom is what we find in the present day theological revolution. When man proclaims the "death of God," is he not simply announcing the end of *a "form" of theological understanding which claimed to be a necessary exigency of the living God?* Is he not thereby desacralizing religion as ideology?

So, the emergence of the free consciousness and its revolutionary understanding of history in all its aspects—science, culture, politics, religion—brings with it the promise (notice, nothing more than a promise) that maybe a new day lies ahead of mankind, if man takes up the task of building it.

Now, let us resume our argument where we left it when we spoke about the new Catholic "utopian" spirituality. This new spirituality is part of the universal symphony of groaning, which has the Spirit as one of the performers (Rom. VIII:26) and hopefully as the conductor. It is obvious that nobody has any certainties in his pocket. Mine is a simple "interpretation" which enjoys the advantage of "fallibility."

But what does this mean? Does it mean that the Christian consciousness has abdicated its specific character and adopted the "fashion" of an epoch in order to become relevant?

Let me suggest a different line of interpretation. The advent of the free consciousness is far from ambiguous. This is why we insist that it only offers a promise, nothing more. The dark side of this freedom is that a man who frees himself from inherited idols can become a prey of the idols which he makes himself. It is Kolakowski again who remarks, and not without a bitter irony—he writes from within a Communist country—that "a rain of gods is falling from the sky on the funeral rites of the one God who has outlived himself. The atheists have their saints and the blasphemers are erecting chapels." [6] We had better not forget the parable of the man who got rid of his demon and kept his house empty. Freedom can become "the obsession for freedom." The loss of our historical memory can give place to alienating illusions about the future. Secularization becomes secularism, revolution becomes tyranny, freedom becomes arbitrariness.

True, the past cannot be our law. *But we cannot dispense with it as grace*. The past as law aborts the future. But the future, left to its own resources, aborts itself. The way to a liberating future depends on our ability to use our memories as a tool, not as a model, to build it, because as Santayana said, only "those who remember the past are not condemned to repeat it."

This is why the new Catholic spirituality is so important. It is an expression of the protest against the past as law, but it remains committed to the past as grace. And consequently *it has possibilities to serve as the midwife in this situation when our present is suffering the pains of childbirth*. From its commitment to mankind's striving for freedom, it derives its universality.

Only after this long preparatory discussion are we prepared to answer the question which was raised: Is this new spirituality now being engendered in the womb of the Roman Catholic Church a planned pregnancy or a bastard? Is it an occasion for joy or a cause for embarrassment? In short, we ask in what ways is the magisterium of the church consciously contributing to the life and growth of this new form of the Catholic faith which embodies religion as utopia?

[6] L. Kolakowski, *op. cit.* pp. 325–326.

The first thing which attracts one's attention is Pope Paul's increasingly greater feeling of pain and anxiety.[7] It is impossible to avoid the impact of his constant references to the crisis which threatens the Church of Rome with subversion and which "could (have a) result fatal not only to its historical balance (the church), but to the glory of the name of Christ, as well, and also to the salvation of many, many souls. . . ." (April 21, 1969).

His feelings and anxiety are born from a precise understanding of the meaning of the new spirituality's tendencies. The problem does not lie in the fact that it is new. The new can very often be the blossoming of the bud, the full realization of tendencies already latent in a previous period. If this were the case, it would serve to vindicate the church's claim of perennial vitality.

But, as we indicated before, the new spirituality, far from claiming to be a new expression of the old, says that there is no way to the new through a developmental process, but rather only through death and resurrection. This is why Pope Paul describes it as subversive and dangerous to the historical balance of the church. The lines of conflict become clearer if we see the model of self-understanding held by Pope Paul which is being subverted by the new one.

Time has always been one of the most troublesome problems for Roman Catholic theology and ecclesiology. How can the church and the truth remain identical with themselves if they change? That which is true cannot change; that which changes cannot be true.

The only solution for the conflict between identity and change was to see the church as located in time but with-

---

[7] I examined the papal statements as they are published by SEDOC— (Documentation Service) Editora Vezes Limitada, Petropolis, RJ, Brasil. The translations from the Portuguese to English are mine. Since I believe that most of those who will be reading this essay do not read Portuguese, I will simply indicate after the quote, between parenthesis the date of the papal audience and, when necessary, other information. The reader will then be able to go to the English sources if he wishes.

out being historical herself. History is provisional. And the truth embodied in the church was not provisional and relative. This solution was preserved in the very suggestive image of the church as an ark floating on the waters of history. Indeed, Paul, as he addressed the Latin-American bishops, recalled this image, indicating how central it is for his view of the church's self-understanding: "From the height of the mystical ark, the church . . ." (August 24, 1968).

The unmistakable influence of Plato in determining how the church understood herself had this result: The only possible forms of change which she came to recognize were those which could be expressed as a logical unfolding or the deepening of the human understanding of an eternal truth already in her possession.

Obviously, this solution simply served to cover a problem which could not be avoided. How could the church's sense of identity subsist at the costly price of ignoring her own history?

In the nineteenth century, the wave of history could no longer be resisted without serious risk. How to deny the weight of evidence? Impossible.

The *Syllabus Errorum* is one of the last dams erected by the church to withstand the tidal waves, and it failed. The crucial problem was raised once again: How to reconcile identity with historical change? Up to that moment, the church had seen herself as a building: solid and changeless. Inside, eternity; outside, time.

Newman abandoned this paradigm. He saw that it presented more problems than solutions. And he suggested a new one, the organism. Organism is identity in change; indeed, identity which requires change. But, as in an organism, all changes are nothing more than the natural and necessary *development* of the *seminal form* which was its beginning and remains as its vital principle. So with the church. Her history is the organic development of the latent tendencies implanted in her by her Founder.

Now change is no longer the spectrum of death but can be understood as the expression of a living organism, always identical with itself, always growing towards more vital forms of life and truth. There are no interruptions or leaps. The present must remain consistent with the past. And the future will be consistent with the past, also.

The past, therefore, is the permanent model for the future. In the language of the computers, it is the "memory" which "programs" change. The past is master; the future is servant. And, of necessity, the past is the law of the present.

It is an irony of history that very often the heresies of yesterday become the truths of the present. When the paradigm of the organism was suggested by Newman, it was branded as heresy. Today, however, it is the official model which informs the official pronouncements of the church of the Second Vatican Council. In the pronouncements of Pope Paul it is an omnipresent element which determined his reading of church history, of human history, his social ethic and, ultimately, his theory of knowledge. This paradigm is the two-edged sword for the defense of the tradition and the fight against those who want to subvert it.

How is it possible to change without losing one's identity? The new emerging spirituality, as we indicated before, believes that one has to be free to rewrite one's own biography if one is to remain alive. The old structure has to die in order to make possible the resurrection of life under revolutionized forms. This is what it means to be free.

The paradigm of organism, however, definitely forbids such a thing. The past must remain as the dominating form, as the master. "As the tree is the development of the seed," remarks Paul, "the history of the church, the process which deepens and widens the seminal elements of evangelical origin, without altering them, without corrupting them, without changing them, leading them to perfect realization . . ." (May, 1969).

"The church needs to remain coherent with her authentic and vital tradition, from which new expressions of her

perennial vitality will come to life, as blossoming branches"
(April 21, 1969).

As with the body, taken in a strictly biological sense
(because for man it is a sociological category, also), all
changes are intended to preserve its form (biology does not
know about death and resurrection), so with the church: her
past form is the law of change. All possible changes aim at its
preservation. From the standpoint of organism, to speak
about a new form is the same as subversion; it implies the end
of life.

Therefore, the form of the church cannot be anything but eternal. She "is the same today, as yesterday as she
will be tomorrow . . ." (June 30, 1968). Indeed one cannot
live "as if it were possible to dispense with the church, since
she is derived from the constitutional principles established by
Christ Himself" (August 7, 1969).

The paradigm of organism provides the justification
for a legal structure: the constitutional principles of the
church are in a direct line with Christ. The functional subor-
dination of change to the traditional form of the church, as
identical with the one originally given by Christ, means neces-
sarily that "the church needs that charity and obedience maintain and strengthen her unity and structure."

And then Paul speaks about the "organic harmony
of charity" (April 21, 1969), a poetic expression which can be
translated as *love is subordinated to form*. Consequently, "the
church is an extremely ordered, hierarchical, organized, and
moralist society. Everything in her is foreseen, classified, and
determined" (September 25, 1969). The fact that in the
church everything is already foreseen indicates that her form
is given by the past, that the past is her law.

We are not specifically concerned with Paul's ecclesiology. But ecclesiology articulates in a conscious level the
unconscious structure which upholds it. His ecclesiology is
built upon a past which has been promoted to ontology. And

ontology, from the standpoint of the sociology of knowledge, says very little about the *ontos,* but is a symptom for us to penetrate in order to get at the logic of the consciousness which supports it. It reveals the rules which control the operation whereby this consciousness "constructs" its world. What is specific of the consciousness which gives to the past the density of ontology is that it believes to be speaking *sub specie aeternitatis.* It claims that its thought is not "interpretation," that is, thought historically conditioned, but perennially valid truth.

Thus, the pope speaks about the *philosophia perennis* of the church (August 24, 1968), and about "the formulas with which the church . . . sealed the dogma in order to pass it through the centuries, carefully preserved, always identical . . ." (April 31, 1968).

If this is the world of the church, *what is the content of the Christian consciousness?* The pope answered it is the "traditional" (March 5, 1969).

It is along these lines that faith is defined as the contemplation of the "objective complex of sublime truths" (June 5, 1968), which constitute the ideal world revealed by the normative past.

The Christian life, therefore, is seen as "the permanent passage from the ideal order" to the historical. When one is so sure about the "ideal world," ethic cannot be anything different from an ethic of principles, absolutes, "which binds our conscience forever and in all circumstances." (From the report of the committee appointed by the pope to indicate what corrections were to be made in the New Dutch Catechism.) It is here that we have to locate the whole problem of natural law and its specific case as it appears in the *Humanae Vitae.*

A consciousness which is wholly determined by the past obviously cannot feel at home amidst uncertainty and search. In the speeches of Pope Paul, one finds a recurring theme, the nostalgia for a time when man had certainties.

The modern mentality, subversive of the certainties of faith, he comments, "tells you that truth is not immobile, that it is not definitive, that it is not sure" (April 3, 1968). And when he lists the various modern tendencies which contest the *philosophia perennis,* such as "secularization, demythologization, desacralization, global contestation and, finally, atheism . . ." (June 12, 1968), he never considers the possibility that maybe the problem is with the church's "interpretation" of the past which transforms it into metaphysics. And this because the voice of the church is never "interpretation" but *philosophia perennis,* "dogma," an "objective complex of sublime truths."

Theologians and preachers may try to interpret what the church says, but the "memory of the church, in itself, is not interpretation, but contemplation"—the platonic anamnesis—of the ideal world.

So, the explanation of contestation is that it is due to man's irrationality. "Why," he asks, "do so many men . . . say the contrary (of what the church says)? We answer: It is because they do not use their intelligence according to the authentic laws of thought in the search for truth . . ." (June 12, 1968). What are these laws? Those "revealed" by the past.

Thus, the past becomes the law of the whole thinking process within the church. It determines the form and content of what can be thought. This is why, if theologians want to be considered authentic, they must "remain as intelligent disciples of the magisterium of the church . . . which was established by Christ as the guardian and interpreter of His eternal truth, by the operation of the Holy Spirit" (August 24, 1968). The consciousness of a man of faith, therefore, is forbidden from trying to rewrite its own biography. It lives, in the words of Dr. Lehmann, a "photoelectric" life.

This explains the recurrent attempts which one finds in the papal declarations to detract from the Second Vatican Council any intentions of structural changes. "One spoke . . . and still speaks about the 'structures' of the church," said Paul in his audience of January 15, 1969. "But this is nothing but the impersonal and outward transformation of the building. . . ."

"The first and most important transformation that the Council intended . . . was the moral, personal and inward renewal . . ." *The form remains the same—but it is given a new life.* Not death and resurrection but an old organism which becomes young again. Through this emphasis on inner life it is both possible to keep on speaking about renewal and to avoid the subversive critique which presses the church in the direction of rewriting her own biography.

When social issues are at stake, the result is similar. Once organism is taken as the model for the understanding of what is involved in the liberation of man, one is led, inevitably, to an ethic which postulates changes (yes, they are needed!) *provided* they will not imply any conflict with the powers that define the structure or forms of a given society. The goal is "social regeneration" and not social revolution.

The reader must be reminded again that we are dealing with all these issues because we want to find the structure of consciousness which determines the specific organization of the various themes which they contain. It is the general structure which provides the hermeneutical principle for the understanding of any document. For instance: when one reads Paul's encyclical *Populorum Progressio,* it makes a radical difference if the hidden linguistic structure which *supports* it is taken into consideration or not. The same is true in trying to understand Paul's statements about ecumenism or any other themes.

Notice then that the problem does not relate to specific issues, pronouncements, and questions. What is at stake is the issue of hermeneutics: what is the paradigm according to which we read our past? A consciousness is not free or oppressed because of words like freedom and oppression. It is on the structural level that the freedom of consciousness is decided.

My personal "interpretation" of the problem is that

the oppressed consciousness is the one which is under the be-witchment of the past; which lives in a world "defined" by the dead definitions which are legitimized as metaphysics, which become the laws of the present, which become the models of the future. Definitions which, precisely because they are defi-nitions, imply that history has come to its end. Definitions which "program" man in a way structurally similar to the bio-logical "programing" which controls animals.

The result of our analysis of Paul's pronouncements shows that—to the extent which they are regulated by the logic of organic development—they establish that the past is master over man and that man, consequently, remains in a sit-uation of unfreedom.

This is the reason why the new Catholic spirituality cannot be considered as anything other than a bastard child. The new thrusts of Catholicism are considered by Paul as sub-versive of the biography of its mother and as a problem to be solved. The immense variety of utopian *themes* in the docu-ments of the magisterium remain as new patches on old clothes. Because an objective analysis does not reveal any signs of change *structurally*.

We should not avoid value judgments of this kind. It is only from the standpoint of our values that we will be able to orient ourselves vis-à-vis the struggle between two different types of spirituality.

Our commitment to the biblical horizons poses a question for us: Does faith live by the contemplation of the model of organism, or by the biblical vision of death and res-urrection? Although the question already suggests the answer, it will have to be answered over and over again. It is not an idle question. What is at stake is whether faith perpetuates the oppressed consciousness of man or whether it liberates it.

Pilgrim for Peace

Gordon C. Zahn

Dr. Zahn, a professor of sociology at the University of Massachusetts, is best known for his studies on the relationship of church and state on issues of war and peace.

He is the author of *German Catholics and Hitler's Wars; In Solitary Witness: The Life and Death of Franz Jagerstatter; War, Conscience, and Dissent; The Military Chaplaincy: Role Tension in the Royal Air Force.*

Dr. Zahn is president of the American Pax Association, and is on the national councils of such organizations as the Fellowship of Reconciliation, SANE, and the Catholic Peace Fellowship.

61

In the first week of his pontificate, Paul VI made his position clear: one of the major tasks of the papacy, he told diplomatic representatives to the Vatican, is the strengthening of peace as based on "the four pillars of truth, justice, love, and liberty" and he added, "we intend to do all we can in this field." This theme was made even more explicit in his first encyclical (*Ecclesiam Suam,* August 1964), traditionally the vehicle for each new pope's "state of the church" assessment. "Regarding the great and universal question of world peace, we say at once that we shall feel it specially incumbent upon us not merely to devote a watchful and understanding interest, but also to entertain a more assiduous and efficacious concern." Later in that same document he declared his readiness "to intervene, where an opportunity presents itself, in order to assist the contending parties to find honorable and fraternal solutions for their disputes."

It is entirely appropriate, then, that some attempt be made to review the record of these past several years to see how successful Paul VI has been in maintaining these laudable intentions and bringing them to fruition. For these have been years of continuing strife and ever-present danger of greater strife. The dreadful war in Vietnam has held center stage, if only by virtue of its cost in lives and devastation; but other wars and conflicts, along with Vietnam, have made of these years one of the most depressing and disillusioning periods of human history. So much so, in fact, that the pope himself was moved to speak (in that same month which brought his hopeful offer to intervene) of "this frightening phenomenon: the crumbling of those basic principles on which peace must be founded." Things were to get much worse before there would be any promise (and that a very faint one indeed) that this "crumbling" might be halted in time to spare mankind the horrors of another world war.

By saying this, of course, we have already established that Paul's pontificate has been a failure if measured by the success he has had in restoring the world to the ways of peace. The reasons for this failure will concern us later in this discussion. What must be said here, however, is that the failure —desperate though it has been—is not due to any weakness or inconsistency in the pope's commitment to the objectives he set. Quite the contrary. Almost every one of his writings, speeches, and official actions has carried some clear references to his overriding concern for world peace. "Making men brothers," defined by him as the Christian mission in the world of today, was to lead him to some truly precedent-shattering moves. But even these were not to bring him the success he sought. At least not yet.

The consistency of his thinking finds dramatic illustration in the close similarity between his first major papal utterance, the 1963 Christmas message, and the December 1967 decision to set aside each New Year's Day as a "Day of Peace." Both pronouncements, and most of the other formal and informal messages issued in the years between, stress five major themes which, taken together, can be read as Paul VI's platform for peace.

First is the exaltation of the ideal of peace itself and its direct (to Paul inescapable) link to the spirit and mission of Christ and the church. In his remarks at the Rome airport as he left for New York to address the United Nations, he declared that his trip had "no other purpose than to encourage, support and bless the efforts of men of goodwill which are directed toward safeguarding, guaranteeing, and strengthening universal peace." "The world," he went on, "expects and asks for peace. The world needs peace. The world demands a real, stable, and lasting peace after the sufferings of war which have deranged our century, after the immeasurable grief which devastated mankind." Recapitulating the effects of his trip upon his return to Rome, he returned to this theme: "Ours has been a mission of peace. Nothing else was intended. There was no other motive to this trip of ours. We have been pilgrims of peace."

It must be said, however, that this celebration of the ideal and symbolism of peace is somewhat weakened by being placed in the context of the pope's insistence that it must be tied to "truth," "justice," and "freedom" and must rest upon the "union of minds" or "internal peace of heart" which arises out of an acceptance of the true moral order. No one can find fault with this impressive set of prerequisites taken singly or as a group. Unfortunately, as they come through in the papal statements, they threaten to restrict the hope for an effective and operative peace to an all but unattainable order of perfection. It would be far more realistic to present international peace and the renunciation of war as the essential precondition from which these other goods would then emerge and develop. There are times, too, when Paul's words seem to imply the need for something approaching a world-wide conversion to a single value system (presumably Christian and Catholic) as a necessary antecedent to the peace ideal he proposes. That any such implication of religious narrowness, if present, is not intended may be seen in his Bombay address to non-Christians in which he calls them to united efforts "toward achieving a true communion among all nations," a union, as he sees it, which "must be built on the common love that embraces all and has its roots in God, who is love."

A far more crucial weakness lies in the frequent intrusion of warnings and reservations against what he chooses to regard as "pacifism" and "pacifist rhetoric." At times these references border upon gratuitous slurs; always they reveal a shocking carelessness in definition of the critical terms. Although one finds this lack of terminological discrimination most glaringly revealed in the December 1967 statement (to be quoted at a later point), it was already there as early as 1963 when he took occasion to warn that "True peace is not that hypocritical propaganda aimed at lulling the adversary to sleep and concealing one's own preparation for war. Peace does not consist in pacifist rhetoric that refuses the indispensable, patient and which [sic] tiresome negotiations [which?] are the only efficacious means."

Not only do such simplistic characterizations carry implications which could detract from or undermine the total and active commitment to the ideal of peace the pope presumably sets out to promote, but they also weaken the second major consistent theme that runs through the papal statements —the insistent appeals for effective world disarmament. Understandably enough, this, then, is the core of the pope's message to the Geneva Disarmament Conference (January 1966): "There is, however, no denying that, with every day that passes, it is becoming more and more obvious that no lasting peace can be established among men until there has been an effective general and controlled reduction in armaments." Again, in the pattern-setting 1963 Christmas message, "the arms race" takes its place along with "nationalistic or ideological pride" and "lack of confidence in the methods or in the organizations that have been constituted to render the relations among nations orderly and friendly" as factors to be abolished or at least mitigated if true peace is to be achieved. The Bombay address, too, carried the warning that the needed communion among nations could not be built "on a universal terror or fear of mutual destruction." The 1964 Christmas message finds him voicing alarm over a militarism which is "no longer focused on the legitimate defense of the countries concerned or on the maintenance of world peace, but [which is] tending rather to build up stockpiles of weapons ever more powerful and destructive. . . ." Two years later in his "piercing cry with tears", as he characterized his encyclical *Christi Matri,* this note of alarm was repeated with sharper focus when he listed "the increasing race for nuclear weapons" among the conditions deeply disturbing to the souls of men. Even this was but a mild echo of the dramatic appeal to the United Nations the preceding October which found him describing disarmament as the first among the "roads" leading to the new, peaceful, and truly human history he presented to his hearers as promised by God. "If you wish to be brothers, let the weapons fall from your hands. One cannot love while holding offensive arms."

What must be regarded as the strongest and most universally applicable of all the long series of testimonials for peace was included in a 1968 speech at Bogotá. "We must say and reaffirm that violence is not in accord with the Gospels, that it is not Christian. . . ." It is true, as some will hasten to point out, that this statement, taken in its immediate historical context, is a cautionary plea to the exploited masses of Latin America not to be misled by advocates of violent revolution. If anything, however, this would seem to enhance rather than diminish its more general application. The fact that he chose to frame his message in terms of a moral principle and, moreover, one rooted in Scripture itself cannot be overlooked. *Violence,* not just violence employed by oppressed against oppressor, is "not Christian." If this is true in a situation where a resort to violence would seem to have a most compelling claim to justification, it must certainly be true in all other situations as well.

The third major theme of the papal statements plays upon the need for internationalism and effective international authority. The most explicit manifestation of this concern was the very fact of the papal visit to New York. The presence of the pope at the United Nations said much more than the text of his remarks praising the organization as an edifice which must never be permitted to fall. Certainly this must have been a particularly bitter pill for those American Catholics, including some powerful spokesmen for the church in this country, who have been opposed to having the United Nations on American soil and to having this nation represented in the United Nations' councils.

The development of international institutions, along with the development of doctrine, are presented in *Ecclesiam Suam* as giving greater urgency to the achievement of the Christian mission of making men brothers. This note is again struck in the 1964 Christmas message—presenting international organization as a bulwark against the threatening rise of nationalism and racism.

In a very real sense it is misleading to speak of disarmament and internationalism as separate themes in the pope's peace platform. They are so intimately intertwined with the fourth major theme of development that all three might better be treated as a single unified theme. As early as the 1963 Christmas message, problems of demography and world poverty take a high priority. The following August, in his address to pilgrims at Castel Gandolfo, Paul links the three themes explicitly: "If the security of peoples still rests on the hypothesis of lawful and collective use of armed force, we must recall that security reposes still more on an effort at mutual understanding, on the generosity of loyal mutual trust, on the spirit of colloboration for mutual advantage and for aid, particularly to developing countries." The pope's visit to India in 1964—unquestionably a tremendous educational experience for him in the personal confrontation it forced with the acute problem of overpopulation and its effects—led him to the programmatic recommendation that arms reduction be effected so that at least part of the arms monies could be spent on the alleviation of world poverty. He was to repeat this proposal at the United Nations. In May 1967, Paul issued what may well rank as his major single pronouncement on the international order, the encyclical *Populorum Progressio*. The issue has since become a popular slogan: "The new name for peace is development."

The theme that remains is one of mood than of content. It is the sense of urgency that dominates all of Paul's statements on the subject of peace. Peace is described as "weak and tottering" in these days (December 1963), as a supreme but "fragile" good (August 1964) "threatened" by a situation "which could at any moment produce the spark for a terrible fresh conflict." In *Christi Matri* the urgency reaches an emotional peak: "We cry to them in God's name to stop. Men must come together and work out concrete plans and terms in all sincerity. A settlement should be reached now, even at the expense of some inconvenience or loss, for it may have to be made later in the train of bitter slaughter and involve great loss." Vietnam is most obviously the immediate cause of his pressing concern, but "things" are taking place in other parts of the world as well which furnish cause for his grave fears. Besides the nuclear race already mentioned, there are "the unscrupulous efforts for the expansion of one's own nation, the excessive glorification of one's race, the obsession for revolution, the iniquitous plotting, the murder of the innocent, all of which are potential material for the greatest possible tragedy."

This sense of urgency has given birth to a remarkable series of symbolic gestures that at times seem to border upon impulsive emotionalism or, as the more cynical would have it, calculated press agentry. One thinks, for example, of the headline-making gifts to the poor or servants of the poor —the donation of a papal tiara, the almost off-hand disposal of the custom-built limousine made available for his use on the trip to India. It would be difficult to deny that these were acts of sincere generosity. At the same time, one can see them as teaching a lesson which was most likely not intended in that they served as shocking reminders of the vast gulf between the virtually immeasurable wealth of the church and the abject poverty of great masses of people in the service of whom that church supposedly exists. Placed in this framework, the gift of one tiara becomes a very small token indeed.

Be that as it may, the most impressive and meaningful symbol of Paul VI's concern for and dedication to world peace and brotherhood remains the series of precedent shattering journeys to such distant places as the Holy Land and India (1964), the United States (1965), Portugal and Turkey (1967), South America (1968), and most recently Geneva (1969). In the short span covering less than a decade, this pilgrim for peace has reversed, hopefully for all time, the policy of studied isolation that had become so much a mark of the papacy in a world that has shown a steadily increasing need of spiritual guidance and values.

To dismiss all this as a kind of grand-scale "tourism" or even, as some have charged, as a supercharged publicity campaign designed to improve the image of the church and the papacy, is to miss the point completely. It represents instead a deliberate and highly imaginative decision on the part of Paul VI to assume (or resume?) the role of missionary pilgrim hastening the day of reconciliation among all men. If John XXIII made his lasting contribution by opening windows to let in fresh air, his successor has gone one step further to throw open the door and venture forth. Tangible results may not have matched hopes and expectations, but at least barriers have been lowered and important beginnings have been made.

Each papal trip has been carefully planned and its purposes spelled out for all to see and hear. Paul went to the Holy Land "as an expression of prayer, penance, and renovation" and "to implore divine mercy on behalf of peace among men, that peace which shows in these days how weak and tottering it is." In Bombay, where he was to participate in a ceremonial congress honoring the Eucharist, he invited non-Christians to join forces with him "to work together to build the common future of the human race." His purposes in visiting the United Nations have already been reviewed. As for the Fatima pilgrimage, he named "peace in the world" as his second principal intention (prayers for the unity and freedom of the church constituting the first). After calling upon all men "to strive to be worthy of the divine gift of peace," he continued, "Do not contemplate projects of destruction and of death, of revolution and of suppression, but think rather of projects of mutual strengthening and of solid cooperation." His trips to Turkey and Geneva would end, or at least greatly reduce, the legacy of deep religious conflict within divided Christianity. Nor can one doubt that the trip to Communist Poland, had it taken place, would have been a major effort to find some way to reduce, or at least to bridge, the ideological gap that presents the gravest threat to the future of both church and world.

True, the historic nature of these pilgrimages were matched in Rome by an equally impressive series of contacts with persons representing religions, regimes, and ideologies that previously would not have obtained (nor, most likely, desired) relationships of any kind with the Holy See. However, even with these contacts taken into account, it is the movement outward across oceans and over continents that has been and will undoubtedly remain the most distinguishing "breakthrough" of the new Pauline era.

Why then, we must ask, has all this failed to produce any significant results in terms of reducing the scope and intensity of the conflicts that have continued throughout his reign? The Vietnam war goes on and, until recently, has escalated in its violence and effects. Other wars, some brief and others longer, but all terribly costly, have started and have involved some of the developing nations that have been so much a special concern of Paul VI. Where wars and lesser conflicts have been brought to a halt, however temporary, few would suggest that papal words or interventions were really responsible. The sincerity and consistency of the pilgrim pope's fervent dedication to peace is beyond challenge. Equally beyond challenge is the sad fact that he has had virtually no success in his efforts to turn the world (or, for that matter, even the Catholics who supposedly accept his spiritual leadership) against war.

The reason for this failure is not hard to find. One need only read the full texts of the messages from which the many citations quoted here have been drawn. The answer lies in the studied ambiguity of these pronouncements, the calculated balancing of firm commitment with emasculating reservations and qualifications—all presented with an overlay of formal and abstract terminological niceties that interpose an almost impenetrable barrier between the inspirational idealism of the contents and any meaningfully specific applications that might be proposed to convert the ideals into actuality. To a great extent these are failings endemic to the genre itself; to a lesser, but still significant, extent it has become all too apparent that they can be traced to inherent limitations in Paul's own thinking on the crucial issues of war and peace in our day.

It is nothing new that pronouncements issuing forth from the Chair of Peter are often bogged down in extravagantly elaborated terminology and overly obscure circumlocutions. What we must ask ourselves is whether the church can afford the luxury of such clearly dysfunctional modes of communication any longer. Recent history provides a particularly tragic example in the case of Pius XII. It may well be that some of the statements so triumphantly quoted by that pope's defenders against the Hochhuth indictment of unfeeling silence in the face of genocide actually *were* conceived by Pius XII as strong protests against the Nazi program for the extermination of European Jewry. The trouble is that to find even a hint of the protest against the Final Solution it is necessary to peel away layers of vague and often pietistic effusions. Even then, once the kernel of protest is reached, much of the

desired meaning must be read into the ambiguous verbiage. If
at the time these statements were first issued, neither the Nazi
rulers nor their loyal German Catholic subjects "got the message," we should not be too surprised. Morally elevating platitudes reaffirming the sacred rights of all persons, coupled with
equally abstract and general expressions of regret when these
rights are violated (care being taken, of course, to avoid naming the specific victims or violators!) may be fine as far as they
go. Unfortunately, such platitudes do not go very far in a
world and an era that are capable of producing an Auschwitz.

So, too, with Paul VI and his peace platform. Like
Pius, he never really gets around to "telling it like it is". Statement after statement contains references which, one suspects,
are intended to protest actions or policies relating to Vietnam;
yet in their finished form these references emerge so cushioned
with ambiguous generalities that it has been no problem at all
for those to whom they were presumably directed to ignore,
or even "welcome," the papal intervention. In *Mense Maio*
(May 1965), for example, we have what seems to be a fairly
explicit condemnation that could apply to either or both sides
in the Vietnamese conflict. "In this respect we cannot fail to
raise our voice in defense of the dignity of man and of Christian civilization, we cannot fail to condemn acts of guerilla
warfare and of terrorism, the practice of holding hostages and
of taking reprisals against unarmed citizens." Earlier in the
same encyclical, he had spoken of the "dreadful spectacle in
certain parts of the world" in which "unspeakable sufferings"
were being brought to populations of entire nations by "acts
of war growing in extent and intensity." No one can fault the
pope on the recognition of these evils. Nevertheless, unless he
was prepared to be more explicit in identifying the culprits, he
might have saved himself the time and intellectual energy for
all the impact his words were likely to have.

"Acts of guerilla warfare"—by whom? Obviously
the National Liberation Front, most American Catholics will
assume. But what about the Green Berets and the "special

services" they are performing in teaching the fundamentals of "dirty tricks" warfare? Or, again, which "hostages" does he have in mind—those spirited away by the Viet Cong, or those photographed while being tortured by South Vietnamese captors with grinning American observers in the background? Those "reprisals against unarmed citizens" certainly refer to the hit-and-run terrorism in Saigon and elsewhere; but, in the eyes of many observers throughout the world, it could apply as well to the "torching" of entire villages by Americans. Lidice and Oradour, one German writer has said, are today villages in Vietnam. Is this, perhaps, what Paul VI was trying to tell us too?

Yet, the communications failure is not one of style alone. On other issues, as the church as learned during Paul's reign, papal documents have been anything but ambiguous or obscure. Whether we consider the controversy stirred by a *Humanae Vitae,* the rigid line proclaimed by Rome on clerical celibacy, or even Paul's frequent and spirited defenses of ecclesiastical authority, there is no disposition to "tone things down." Not only is every effort made to spell out the issues as clearly as possible, but the insistence upon conformity and obedience on the part of the Catholic faithful is made a central issue. Not so, however, with the issues of war and peace.

The restraint which robs his words of any really productive impact is probably more institutional than personal, though as we shall see the latter is an important factor too. As long as the papacy jealously guards the fiction of "temporal sovereignty," it will continue to feel bound by the rules of the diplomatic game with the almost inescapable result that, in any apparent clash between the two, papal concern for diplomatic formalities and procedures will take precedence over concerns of the moral order that may be involved. As a result when the pope does choose to speak, his voice is likely to be muted and uncertain.

From time to time Paul has given reason to hope

that he is prepared to abandon that fiction, but to this point that hope has not been fulfilled. True, we have his characterization of himself before the United Nations as "the least invested" of the sovereign powers gathered there, as one who can claim only "a miniscule, as it were symbolic, temporal sovereignty, only as much as is necessary to be free to exercise his spiritual mission, and to assure all those who deal with him that he is independent of every other sovereignty of this world."

This, of course, is the standard rationalization of the arrangement and, in theory at least, it has much to commend it. A counter-argument, however, would hold that by preserving the Vatican's status as a sovereign state among sovereign states, the church becomes, in a sense, dependent upon all other sovereignties with which it seeks to maintain relationships. As the reigns of Pius XII and now Paul VI show only too clearly, the demands of diplomacy have operated more often than not to restrict the freedom of action of the papacy in precisely those issues and areas where a strong moral protest might be in order. If Paul were really prepared to divest himself of all the trappings of temporal sovereignty and assume the role of a stateless pilgrim possessing no status among the princes and principalities of the world—other than that of prophet giving voice to the violated conscience of mankind— his appeals and protests might have far more impact upon world events.

How much more impact will depend in large part upon the personality of the man who occupies the papal throne at any given time. In Paul's case there is reason to doubt whether the change would be all that great. His appeals for peace and his blueprints for the kind of world order which would make for lasting peace have been strong and consistent and, without a doubt, utterly sincere. At the same time he has not shown himself capable of developing that "entirely new attitude" toward war and the evaluation of war called for by the Fathers of Vatican II. Instead one cannot escape the impression of theological rigidity (almost to the point of fixation) tying him to traditional formulations and applications that offer little or no promise of being useful, or even valid, today. The result has been that many of his most stirring pronouncements concerning war and peace come through as little more than the "rhetoric" he ascribes to others and their positions.

It would be too easy to say that here, as in other moral contexts, Paul VI has shown himself to be a "Hamlet" on the papal throne, a pope who seems intent upon balancing each step toward liberalization of the church with at least one step back toward entrenched traditionalism. Actually the problem here is not so much one of direction or consistency as it is one of the perfectionist insistence already noted on the whole package of an ideal social order of "truth, freedom, and justice" as a precondition to an effective and complete rejection of war and the ways of war. Everyone would endorse the vision proposed in the papal message; unfortunately it is also true that both sides to every international conflict will find it possible to justify recourse to military action in terms of the absence of one or another part of the total package.

In this context Paul's rather distorted notion of what a more pacifist stance implies becomes crucial. Even as he calls for a world celebration of the ideal of peace, he feels compelled to express the hope that this will not "favor the cowardice of those who fear it may be their duty to give their life for the service of their own country and of their own brothers." "Peace," he warns, "is not pacifism; it does not mask a base and slothful concept of life, but it proclaims the biggest and most universal values of life: truth, justice, freedom, love."

At the December 1967 press conference where the text of the message containing these fears and warnings was released, officials of the Vatican Secretariat found it necessary to explain that the pope's words were not to be read as a condemnation of conscientious objection; and they supported their clarifying statement by citing both the Pastoral Constitution on the Church in the Modern World and Paul's own *Populorum Progressio*. One can be grateful for such clarification while still deploring the careless papal thinking which made it necessary in the first place. Nowhere is his fear that peace might become the refuge of the coward matched by concern for the far more general problem of men accepting military service as a "duty" without even considering the justice or injustice of the cause for which they will be dying and, of special importance one would think to the Christian, killing. Certainly there are men who are pacifists because of cowardice and sloth, and they are quite properly open to criticism by a pope or anyone else. But this should be balanced by equally strong criticism of the so-called "war lover," the men to be found in all armed forces who are there because they take pleasure in killing others. Just as it would be grossly unfair to condemn all soldiers as "war lovers," so is it unfair to dismiss pacifism and pacifists as cavalierly as Paul VI seems to do.

The tragic thing is that these references are not to be explained away as a matter of semantic carelessness. I suspect that, subsequent clarifications aside, this *is* what pacifism means to him. It follows that he will always be inclined to be unnecessarily hesitant and cautious about offering practical recommendations for action which might seem to foster or endorse the "pacifism" he rejects. If true, this could prove to be a fatal weakness; for the elimination of war, if it is ever to be achieved, will have to begin with specific acts of opposition to war and a general refusal on the part of Christians to participate in or support wars and military operations.

Until Paul VI comes to terms with this, he is likely to find himself stuck at the level of "rhetoric." At the United Nations he declared to the world that "the hour has struck for our 'conversion,' for personal transformation, for interior renewal." He went on to say, "we must get used to thinking of man in a new way; and in a new way also of men's life in common." In a very real sense we can turn his words back on him and suggest that he must somehow free himself (and, having done so, the Catholic community he heads) from the sterile bonds of a medieval theological structure made up of teachings and definitions that have become quite irrelevant to the actuality of modern war. It is not enough to issue the rally call, "No more war, war never again!", and stop there. If "it is peace which must guide the destinies of people and of all mankind," the pope cannot be indifferent to the great masses of Catholics all over the world who pay him and his words little or no heed as they continue to march to the colors of their separate nations.

One would not wish to end this resume on too negative a note. On balance the reign of Paul VI to this point shows more plusses than minuses, at least on issues related to war and peace. There is every reason to hope that if Paul continues in his commitment to peace, his perspective will broaden and the inner dynamism of the movement toward peace will bring him closer to a far more thoroughgoing pacifist stance than he has been willing to contemplate thus far. Just as he made the truly significant shift from the spoken and written word to the symbolism of his world pilgrimages, so we may hope he will make the equally significant move from symbolic gesture to effective act. The critic will insist that it is already too late to restore the papacy to the position where it can again be taken seriously by the peoples of the world and the leaders of nations. That remains to be seen. It is entirely possible that whatever he might choose to do to further the cause of peace may be doomed to fail, just as his efforts until now have failed. Even so, something would have been gained just in making the change in mode and direction. If nothing else, the failure then would be one of a good spiritual battle fought and lost, and no longer that of a religious community and its leadership not measuring up to the challenge because of misdirected effort or inadequate understanding of the moral issues at stake.

Birth Control and Celibacy

Robert G. Hoyt

Mr. Hoyt is editor of the *National Catholic Reporter*. He has contributed articles and essays to, among other publications, *America, Commonweal, The Critic, Informations Catholiques Internationales, Jubilee, Social Order, The Catholic Mind,* and *Ave Maria.* He has served as a vice president of the Catholic Association for International Peace. He has been a member of the Missouri Advisory Committee to the United States Commission on Civil Rights, the Kansas City Human Relations Commission, the board of directors of the Urban League of Kansas City and of the American Benedictine Academy.

The books he has edited include *Issues That Divide the Church, The Birth Control Debate,* and *Special to the N.C.R.*

Paul VI wants very much to be a contemporary pope, to be in touch, to remain, as he described himself in the encyclical on celibacy, "ever intent on the realities of today." In some notable ways he succeeds. Consider, for instance, his appearance at the United Nations in October 1965. One can imagine Pius XII consenting to address the General Assembly, but it is not easy to picture him jetting to New York to make it possible. And, if he had made the trip, he would have projected from the podium his own conception of himself as a divinely appointed instructor in the law of nations. The self-image conveyed by Paul was both more ancient in its roots and more fitting to these times—he was a priestly witness for peace, pleading the cause of man.

Paul's bearing also suits the twentieth century better than that of his mentor Pius. He does not make jokes or poke fun at himself as John XXIII did, but he is often self-deprecatory and shy rather than regal or assertive, and sometimes he can relax. On his return from Uganda in midsummer, 1969, he delighted a crowd of tourists at Castel Gandolfo by executing a little jig to help describe the way African nuns had danced for him.

Even in defending the powers of his office (outside of formal documents), he is not "pontifical"; one feels he is conserving an idea of the papacy rather than an apotheosized image of himself. Though he sorrows vocally over "modern errors," he also pays just tribute to ideas he considers new and good. And the language of his condemnations, while often quite as convoluted as any that has proceeded from the chair of Peter, has often been less harsh than the defensively strident tones of some recent predecessors—witness, for example, the very sharp difference in this respect between *Humanae Vitae* and *Casti Connubii*. Paul's social thought advances boldly beyond the positions announced by *Mater et Magistra* and *Pacem in Terris*. The neo-colonialist order of things holds no sacredness for him; during his reign the Vatican has not attempted to reinstall the Kremlin as chief font of earthly evils or to bring out of retirement the old, self-serving comparisons between "Christian civilization" and "godless communism."

And, finally, Paul reads. When Harvey Cox was in Rome for a Vatican-sponsored symposium of theologians and sociologists, he was startled by a remark the pope addressed to him personally during a group audience; it was, in effect, "We don't agree with you, but we have read your work." That isn't something a youngish American Baptist writer expects to hear at St. Peter's from the chief papist.

Clearly, then, Paul aspires to be modern. But the real test of contemporaneity for a pope has to be associated with his own conception of the church and the papacy, most of all with the way he confronts the possibilities of change in these institutions. What influence the papacy retains on secular affairs is apt to be directly proportional to the incumbent pope's success or failure in coping with those problems that are thought to be properly his. He will not be considered a man of his own time—and therefore a man to be reckoned with—unless he approaches the ecclesiastical issues that history puts on his agenda in a contemporary spirit. That spirit does not mean going along with every new fad in theology or

churchmanship. It does require of the man who speaks to the
world from Peter's throne that he speak in a way that shows
he has listened, that he is really intent on the *realities* of
today.

Obviously, the papacy has suffered a decline in
prestige from the very high point it reached at the death of
John. That may well have been inevitable. Neither Giovanni
Montini nor any other man could have duplicated the charismatic appeal of Giuseppe Roncalli; perhaps no previous pope
has faced a more difficult set of problems within his own
household than Paul VI has confronted and still confronts.
Yet it can be argued, and will be argued here, that Paul has
failed (not finally, but seriously), precisely because he is not
sufficiently what he would like to be, a contemporary man.
This failure shows up most clearly in his way of dealing with
birth control and celibacy, the two most powerfully divisive issues that have come before him.

Any such judgment reeks of personal bias (as would
an opposite judgment), but I feel no need of going beyond a
declaration of that bias: that is, I disagree with the pope's decisions on these questions. For it is possible to set the decisions themselves to one side, or even to assume that they were
right, and still to argue for the thesis that they exemplify
Paul's failure to be fully present to his time. The thesis does
not merely depend on the fact that the two decisions were un-
popular; wisdom and relevancy aren't always popular. Paul's
failure has to do rather with the approach adopted, the kind
of awareness shown in determining the context of these issues,
the methods of problem-solving and conflict-resolution chosen, the care taken in defining criteria of truth and procedures
of investigation that will produce answers appropriate to the
issues. The underlying assumption is that the church's response to basic questions should produce answers that will, by
their very form, show that the questions were understood, that
they were taken seriously as real questions, and that the investigation and reflection which produced the answers were truly

disinterested. It is characteristic of modern man—and one of the best things about him—that when any man or institution declares a truth, he wants to ask: "How do you know? What did you do to find this out?"

Some day perhaps a properly qualified scholar will bring his analytic tools to bear on the content of *Humanae Vitae* and *Sacerdotalis Caelibatus* and on the processes by which they were produced, looking for answers to the two questions involved; in doing so he will bring out the philosophical presuppositions, the modes of argument, the rhetorical techniques employed. That sort of analysis is neither appropriate to this book nor within my capacity, but I can offer some pointers.

A good place to start is at the edge of things. At one point in *Humanae Vitae* the pope touches lightly on the possible effects on male-female mutuality that might follow if contraception were permitted. Men, he says, may come to think of women as mere instruments of selfish enjoyment, and no longer as their respected and beloved companions.

We are at "the edge of things" because within the structure of the encyclical this comment is merely a peripheral observation, offered in support of the main thesis rather than as proof of it. However, it seems to me wonderfully instructive to reflect on this very fact. For, I submit, the contemporary mind instantly recognizes the point at issue as highly pertinent to the larger argument, and also as an essentially factual question. *Does* the use of contraceptives make women into sex objects? Or does it make possible a humanizing and personalizing of the sexual encounter? Or is it only one factor among many affecting the meaning of sex? These questions are not at all peripheral to the issue of the morality of contraception. And if they are significant questions, their answers ought not to be assumed; nor (most importantly) should it be assumed that in seeking the answers there exists no need of consulting the experience of mankind.

In this connection it is worth noting the amount of vocal exasperation occasioned by this brief passage of the encyclical, despite its carefully tentative phrasing ("the man, growing used to the employment of anti-conceptive practices, *may finally lose* respect for the woman . . ."). It could well be that this exasperation reflects moral insensitivity, an impatience with *any* moral protest against *any* new gimmick or convention that makes life easier and pleasure more accessible. But some of it, I suggest, is based on a profound insight into the epistemological weakness of the encyclical. A debate on the morality of contraception taking place in the seminary classroom forty years ago (if such a debate could have occurred at all) would have seen both sides relying on and restating their fundamental understandings of human nature and of the divine purpose in the making of two sexes. That is not a contemporary approach; people today will not accept the assertion that the use of contraceptives demeans sex unless some kind of effort is made to investigate the testimony of experience. Granted, men and women who have used contraceptives will tend to be defensive about the spiritual-emotional effects, but sociologists have ways of taking such bias into account; that is why disinterested sociological studies can be made even in emotionally charged areas. The methods of empirical science are not infallible, but neither is philosophical reasoning; and, given the availability and refinement of empirical modes of truth-seeking, pronouncements dealing with the right and wrong of behavior which are based on theory and not backed by data become worse than useless. You don't reason to a conclusion about the height of a table if there is a yardstick in the closet. And if you insist on spurning the yardstick you will be suspected not only of having a fixed opinion about the table's height but also of harboring a vested interest in your opinion which will not allow you to test it.

Whether or not this last suspicion is justified in the present instance, it does seem fair to say that the encyclical and the process which led up to it reveal, by default, a distrust of yardsticks—that is, of methods of investigation which require a truth-seeker first to find and then to follow the evidence. The papal birth control commission did hear some experientially based and/or scientifically validated testimony about sex in general and birth control in particular, but it was not authorized to sponsor or even to foster independent research. In any case, the findings of the commission were dismissed by the encyclical in a single sentence. As for the content of the encyclical, the pope reached a definitive conclusion on a many-sided question in all-but-exclusive reliance on the methods of speculative analysis, working on a restricted set of data selected mostly from biology rather than from knowledge-sources closer to the level of human values. Before he approached the psychological, demographic, cultural, sociological facts about contraception, he already "knew" that it was an evil practice—and hence that it *has* to have dehumanizing effects on the male-female sexual exchange.

The tentative phrasing of the latter assertion as it appears in the encyclical may reflect some awareness of the methodological error involved. Tentative or not, it is a tip-off. It starts a train of thought leading to the conclusion that the question the pope started out to answer was never really a question for him, and—more pertinently—that he instinctively rejected alternative methods of inquiry into the issue because the results of these kinds of investigation could not be controlled in advance. (Even to admit the possible relevance of psychology and sociology in measuring qualitative aspects of behavior is to work a change in the meaning you give to "morality.")

Distrust of inquiry is not only alien and unpersuasive to the contemporary mind, it is a sure defense against becoming a modern man. When it is the pope who evidences such an attitude, he constitutes himself a barrier between the church and the realities of today. Such a posture suggests that for the church there is no *inner* risk, no adventure, no novelty in the enterprise of being Jesus in the here and now; that Jesus

is being used as the Certificator of judgments on human conduct which are cultural products rather than intimations from
divinity; and that the church's interest is to *control* man rather
than to introduce him to reality.

One does not make so amorphous an entity as "the
contemporary mind" the measure of truth, nor is rational
analysis outmoded as a tool of ethical investigation. Philosophy is no more hair-splitting than sociology is nose-counting.
The writings of Fathers and Doctors of the church are as alive
and relevant as those of Alfred Kinsey and William Masters.
Sex is a complicated thing, and contraception makes a big
change in its meaning. It is very much to the church's credit,
then, that it remains concerned about the moral aspect of
birth control, and it is a significant indicator of callousness on
the part of the "modern world" that it no longer sees any
problem. In short, it's very likely that a truly disinterested and
genuinely interdisciplinary study of the morality of contraception would come up with complicated results surprising to
both sides of the controversy.

Of itself, the birth control issue ought never to have
become centrally important and cruelly divisive in the life of
the church; but history does not behave with rational good
taste. Once the issue became so heavily freighted with symbolic significance, it almost demanded (says hindsight) a response which would show that the church was really curious
about the truth of the matter, instead of perceiving it chiefly
as a threat to ecclesiastical authority. It asked rather, for a liberating and imaginative mode of solution. And that is the contribution Paul VI might have made—to join the church's inherited wisdom with modernity's new techniques and new
kinds of awareness; to *expect* to be surprised, to *offer* the results instead of imposing them. To ask this is to ask a great
deal. But there is no easy way of being a contemporary pope.

Despite the seriousness of the birth control debate
within the Catholic Church, it has always had a touch of the
ridiculous about it, since most of the heavyweight thinking

and passionate polemics it has occasioned have been carried out by celibates. Today there is a positive tone in the church's official teaching about sexuality; sex is presented primarily as a gift to be appreciated rather than as a trap to be feared. Documents like *Humanae Vitae,* however, tend to strengthen the suspicion that while celibate churchmen talk eloquently about the glory of sex, many of them are uncomfortable with the thought that people actually do take off their clothes and celebrate this glory.

This same suspicion extends to the discussion of celibacy itself. There are grounds for thinking that there is in the minds of some prelates a residual revulsion over the image of a man's hands lifting the Host in the morning after having caressed a woman's body in the night. The language of Paul VI's *Sacerdotalis Caelibatus,* in the passages dealing with the "sad state" and the "spiritual and moral collapse" of priests who have left the ministry for marriage, gives at least a hint that old-style Catholic puritanism retains some influence with him. But this is not a line of thinking that can be pursued very far, since it is so easy in reading the psychic states of another man to find projections of one's own—and since what strikes one observer as Manichean in flavor may seem healthy and normal to another.

Apart from such subjectivisms, it is clear that what has already been said about Paul's handling of the birth control issue applies also to his policy on celibacy. That is, he can be charged with neglecting ways of investigating the subject that might have turned up relevant data.

Is there, for instance, a cultural component in the meaning of celibacy? It is said that in some African cultures celibacy does not speak at all of asceticism (the traditional rationale for it in the West); neither does it have an eschatological signification, an effect of pointing to the coming of the Kingdom (a more recent grounding for the practice). And, finally, the supposed apostolic advantage in the freedom from family cares which celibacy confers is more than canceled out in such cultures, since the celibate man is regarded as unmanly, not worth listening to. The origins and human worth of these attitudes are subject to evaluation by the methods of cultural anthropology, but there is no evidence in *Sacerdotalis Caelibatus* that the pope has heard its testimony on the topic.

In fact, *any* testimony likely to threaten the established tradition is in effect ruled out in advance. In *Humanae Vitae* the recommendations of the papal birth control commission were discredited because in its deliberations "certain criteria of solutions had emerged which departed from the moral teaching on marriage proposed with constant firmness by the teaching authority of the church." So also with celibacy; the church must not "be regarded as having followed for centuries a path which, instead of favoring the spiritual richness of individual souls and of the People of God, has in some way compromised it, or of having stifled, with arbitrary judicial prescriptions, the free expansion of the most profound realities of nature and of grace." Therefore, though the pope himself proposes a study of the life circumstances of married non-Catholic clergy who want to enter the church and continue in the ministry, any such study must not "prejudice the existing discipline regarding celibacy"; research and discussion on celibacy should be aimed solely at "defense of the spiritual meaning and moral value of virginity and celibacy." You can ask any question you like, provided it fits an answer already accepted. Not, therefore, "Is mandatory clerical celibacy a good thing?" but, "Why is celibacy so great?". One can sympathize with the pope's complaint that the very raising of a question about the worth of celibacy automatically weakens its attraction (". . . tears down that vigor and love in which celibacy finds security and happiness"). But the question is there and it cannot be erased because it is disruptive, least of all by a deliberate regression to obscurantism.

Critics of *Sacerdotalis Caelibatus* have objected not only to the impression it gives of reciting predetermined answers from the past but also to the context in which it treats the issue of celibacy. Or, rather, to the lack of context. In 1966 Pope Paul himself wrote to an Italian study week on pastoral *aggiornamento:* "No one can be unaware that a wave of doubt, malaise and uneasiness today besets many priests." Yet as Jacques Duquesne observes (*A Church Without Priests,* Macmillan, 1969), "Perhaps this wave is stronger than Roman officials realize." He records, for example, that between 1960 and 1966 more than ninety books on the crisis of the priesthood were published in the French language alone. Along with many others, he concludes from his studies and interviews that celibacy is not at the root of this crisis.

To speak generally, priests are not leaving the priesthood in order to marry; rather they are marrying because they have left the priesthood. The reasons for their disenchantment with the ministry are complex and varied, so much so as to be beyond summation here. The point is that except for some passages exhorting bishops to be kind and fatherly to their priests, nothing the pope says in treating of celibacy indicates awareness of the reasons why so many priests are unhappy. On the contrary—and this in my view is the most central criticism to be made on the topic—he is unaware that his own way of responding to the celibacy crisis typifies an ecclesiastical mode of decision-making which is among the most profound sources of priestly unrest. And, once again, the failure is one either of lack of insight into contemporary man, or of unwillingness to adjust to contemporary values though adaptation is possible.

What I am talking about is not the decision conveyed in the encyclical or the quality of its argumentation, but rather the fact that it constitutes a verdict reached without a hearing. The pope says he has been attentive to current studies of celibacy; yet he all but acknowledges, both in the encyclical and elsewhere (letter to Cardinal Tisserant, Oct. 10, 1965) that the sole purpose of his own study has been to find new ways of showing priests why they should value celibacy and how they should safeguard it. In this respect it is even more significant that Paul forbade discussion of celibacy in the fourth session of the Council: "Public debate," he wrote, "is not opportune on this subject which is so important and which demands such profound prudence." The subject was again ruled off the agenda for the first meeting of the World Synod of Bishops in 1967. Such procedures can only confirm the experience-based conviction of many priests, conservatives as well as progressives, that no matter how great their problems, no matter how honestly and humbly they describe their situation and ask for help, they are not going to be heard, nor will they have opportunity to share in formulating the policies which determine the conditions of their lives and ministries.

Only a decade or so ago it might have been appropriate (or seemed appropriate) for a pope to say: "This question is very important and very delicate; therefore I will settle it alone." But time makes a real difference in human affairs, and today that conclusion does not follow from that premise. The church has not been converted into a democracy, and there are still no constitutional limits on the power of the papacy over ecclesiastical policies. Yet the assertion of unqualified papal authority over questions affecting the vocation and the very identity of papal subjects strikes a jarring note. It contrasts harshly with "secular" developments such as the rise of participatory democracy, the efforts of psychologists and educators to foster personal autonomy, the recognition of the rights of workers to share in fixing the conditions of their work, of women to be recognized as persons, of ex-colonial peoples to assert their national prerogatives. These developments have been not only acknowledged by the church as realities but praised as steps toward realization in society of the Christian understanding of man.

By his approach to the celibacy question (among other problems), Paul has in effect denied the relevance of all this to the life of the church. That may be inevitable. A different course taking modern values into account would have worked a real change in the church and in the papacy, and few men who inherit power are strong enough to give it up or share it, or wise enough to conceive new ways of exercising their authority. However understandable, Paul's reluctance is a sad thing. One cannot argue *a priori* that the results following from a procedure admitting wider participation (or at least more public dialogue) would have been different; or, if different, wiser. On the other hand, there is absolutely nothing in Catholic tradition which required the pope to foreclose debate in the Council and the synod, or which prevented him from authorizing research in the relevant disciplines, or which ruled out the possibility of limited experimentation with a married clergy in some cultures and circumstances. Granting again that no one of these steps nor any combination of them would have guaranteed a "right" decision, neither did the procedure actually followed; for no one, not the most ardent defender of papal powers, suggests that the pope's decision on such a question could be labeled infallible. Because it depended for its legitimacy almost wholly on the pope's authority, the decision appeared as authoritarian, unilateral, anti-collegial. There was nothing in the encyclical or in the steps that led to its issuance to remind anyone of the Council's brave words about the church as the People of God, about collegiality, about the right of all to be heard in the councils of the church, or (most of all) the right of the human person to realize himself in the acts of knowing and choosing and in his life in community. Given the deep roots of modern man's commitment to these values, given the malaise among priests rising from their sense of being mere instruments of their superiors, it seems to me that Pope Paul's mode of deciding the celibacy question and promulgating his decision was imprudent—contrary to the church's best interests, likely to produce discontent and rebellion much worse than the conditions which brought the issue up for resolution.

The only way to soften such judgments is to stress again that they are made after the fact, by the wisdom of hindsight; and, perhaps more importantly, that one cannot now see the difficulties that would have risen to view if other policies had been followed. It is not self-evident, for example, that the papacy would have gained in prestige if Paul had "given way" on birth control and celibacy. It is not certain—in fact, it seems unlikely—that progressive Catholics would have observed a decent restraint in victory; quite possibly they would have pressed mercilessly for further, more radical changes in Catholic doctrine and polity, to the point of driving traditionalists into schism. Granting all this, and granting the great burdens of history and responsibility inhibiting any pope from accepting basic, precedent-setting change, it still seems to be clear that in his response to these great issues, Pope Paul has misread the signs of the times. Because of his failure of vision, the fulfillment of the promise of Vatican II will be long delayed, and perhaps never realized as it might have been.

Paul's Contribution to Ecumenism

Robert McAfee Brown

Dr. Brown was an official Protestant observer
at the sessions of the Second Vatican Council.
His book *An American Dialogue*, which he
coauthored with the late Jesuit priest Gustave
Weigel, was considered at the time of its
publication an ecumenical breakthrough. He is
today America's best known ecumenist.
Currently a professor at Stanford University, he is
the author of such works in ecumenism as
Observer in Rome, The Ecumenical Revolution,
and *The Spirit of Protestantism*.

Two kinds of problems beset any Protestant evaluation of papal contributions to ecumenism. The first is related to the stance of the evaluator, who will naturally take a positive view of papal contributions that reform the church and Christian relations in ways consonant with his own presuppositions, and a negative view of papal actions that seem to be at variance with the "ongoing Reformation" to which the Protestant is pledged. A problem noted is in part a problem overcome, but only if there is coupled with it the conviction, here presupposed, that a true ecumenical attitude does not wish to make another church conform to one's own, but rather to urge all churches to rise to what is greatest in their own traditions, convinced that such fidelity will draw separated Christians closer to one another, rather than driving them farther apart. True reform, commitment to the belief in *ecclesia semper reformanda*—since Vatican II a Roman Catholic as well as a Protestant principle—can only enhance ecumenical understanding, leading those who practice it closer to the time when the now-divided Christian family is again one.

The second problem is the problem of what we mean when we use the word "ecumenism." At least two basic understandings of the term are important in what follows, and to whatever degree they could once be separated in the past, they can no longer be separated today. We can distinguish between ecumenism as an intramural concern for the reunion of divided Christian bodies, and ecumenism as an extramural concern for the joint action of Christian bodies, whether reunited or not, in the contemporary world.[1] Another way to make the distinction is to refer to ecumenism as a subject matter *per se,* in contrast to ecumenism as a perspective that can be brought to bear on all other subjects.

The distinction is important in any assessment of papal contributions to ecumenism, for in the former case the subject matter could be fairly delimited to include only papal words or actions dealing with Christian reunion, whereas in the latter case virtually *any* papal action could be assessed for "ecumenical" implications in the world at large. As the following examination will make clear, both the narrower and the wider definition will have to be employed almost interchangeably, for the more Christians have pondered their intramural relationship with one another, the more they have been forced to confront their relationship with the entire *oikoumene.* Conversely, the more Christians have tried to cope with the vast range of problems confronting the contemporary world the more they have been forced to find ways of engaging in that confrontation together. Traffic runs both ways on this particular street. To take the most obvious example, if at one time a certain view of papal authority led to a specific attitude on birth control, it is now patently clear (assessing the reaction to *Humanae Vitae*), that a specific attitude toward birth control is leading to a new and radically different understanding of

[1] The latter definition of the term is linguistically justifiable when one remembers that the earliest meaning of *oikoumene* was simply "the inhabited world," quite apart from any theological or ecclesiastical connotations. The latter type of ecumenism is currently described as "secular ecumenism," a useful but somewhat misleading term, since it suggests that there might be a "sacred ecumenism" in contrast to it.

papal authority. *Humanae Vitae* has both kinds of "ecumenical" implications, i.e., it influences the relationship between Roman Catholicism and other Christian churches, and it influences, for better or worse, the stance that all Christians take toward the contemporary world.

With these considerations in mind, we can examine some of the contributions of Paul VI to the ecumenical scene.

Even before the second session of Vatican II convened (the first under Paul's pontificate), Pope Paul had informed the Roman Curia of its own imminent reform. Although such action might seem to be an exclusively intramural Roman Catholic affair, the word was eagerly heard by outsiders as well, for "reform of the Curia" had been an item high on the agenda of the reformation movements in the sixteenth century, and Adrian VI had pointed out the need for internal reform in the high places of the Vatican. Somehow in the intervening centuries, the step had not been taken and although the events of Vatican II postponed the original Pauline timetable, specific reforms were proposed and put into effect on August 15, 1967 in the apostolic constitution *Regimini Ecclesiae Universae*.[2]

There have also been a few tentative steps toward the "internationalization of the Curia," which is clearly essential in the modern world, and it will probably be by the degree to which this is achieved, more than by the specific structural changes, that the entrance of the Roman Catholic Church into the pluralistic, diverse world of twentieth-century man will be assured.

A number of papal actions at Vatican II were ecumenically significant. It may turn out in retrospect that Paul's most important contribution to ecumenism was the tone and substance of his opening allocution at the second session of

[2] Cf. *The Pope Speaks*, vol. 12, no. 4, pp. 393–420, for the text. Hereafter such references will be cited as *TPS*, 12, 4: 393–420.

Vatican II, on September 29, 1963. Up to that point there had been no "official" acknowledgement of Roman Catholic responsibility for the sin of Christian division, and it had appeared to the non-Catholic that he was supposed to bear full responsibility for a divided church, the Catholic attitude being that of the indulgent mother who would welcome back the properly penitent wayward child. Such an attitude was scarcely conducive to mutual esteem, and it was a breakthrough of incalculable importance when Pope Paul said to the non-Catholic "observers" at the Council:

> If we are in any way to blame for that separation, we humbly beg God's forgiveness. And we ask pardon too of our brethren who feel themselves to have been injured by us. For our part, we willingly forgive the injuries which the Catholic Church has suffered, and forget the grief endured during the long series of dissensions and separations.[3]

In his audience with the observers some weeks later, Pope Paul made the point again: "In Our speech of September 29, We ventured to give the first place to Christian forgiveness, mutual if possible. 'We grant pardon and ask it in return.' " [4]

The fact that such words have become an ecumenical commonplace in 1970 is precisely because Paul took the lead in 1963. Up to that time, such declarations of Catholic need for forgiveness were confined to individual Catholic theologians, but as a result of the papal allocution the theme became securely embedded in the conciliar decree *On Ecumenism,* passed at the end of the third session.

The papal relation to the decree *On Ecumenism* is somewhat ambiguous. On the one hand, there is no doubt of papal support for the themes enunciated in it, or of Pope

---

[3] Cited in Küng, Congar, and O'Hanlon, eds., *Council Speeches of Vatican II* (Glen Rock, N.J.: Paulist Press, 1964), pp. 146–147.

[4] For a fuller account of this meeting, cf. the author's *Observer in Rome* (New York: Doubleday & Company, 1964), p. 80.

Paul's commitment to foster better relationships between Roman Catholicism and other Christian bodies. But just before the decree in its final form was to be voted on, Pope Paul introduced nineteen changes into the text, too late for discussion by the Council fathers, who thus had to accept or reject the amended text without debate. Although only one of the modifications introduced a substantive change in the text (that Protestants "seek" God rather than "find" Him in Holy Scripture), there was considerable negative response to the action, which appeared to foster "papalism" rather than "collegiality," suggesting a view of pope as superior to council, rather than of pope and council working together. This mood was reinforced when the pope, in his closing address to the third session, bestowed on Mary the title *Mater ecclesiae,* Mother of the church, even though the bishops had earlier felt the title to be inappropriate. Ecumenical apprehensions were further increased when a decision was made, with papal support, to postpone a vote on the declaration on religious liberty until the fourth session, an action that appeared to many progressive bishops (and virtually all non-Roman Catholics) as an attempt to destroy the declaration by delay. The fears, however, were greater than the facts could warrant, for at the final session an admirable decree on religious liberty was overwhelmingly adopted, clearly with papal approval, and its proponents could argue that the text was superior to that offered at the end of session three.[5]

Once again, the notion that the Catholic Church believes in religious liberty for non-Catholics does not seem particularly newsworthy after the event, but it would be hard to measure the ecumenical setback that would have resulted had the vote gone the other way or been very close, or had the document been buried between sessions and never resurrected.

---

[5] For further analysis of these events, and the decree *On Ecumenism* as a whole, cf. the author's *The Ecumenical Revolution,* revised and expanded edition (Garden City, N.Y.: Doubleday & Company, Anchor and Image books, 1969), esp. Chs. 9 and 11, which contain further documentation.

Pressures on the pope from conservatives to oppose the declaration were enormous throughout the Council, and his resistance to those pressures gives him high marks on any ecumenical tally sheet.

Two other conciliar events had specific ecumenical implications. One of these was the worship service that Pope Paul initiated between the Council fathers and the non-Catholic observers during the closing days of the fourth session. Since joint worship had been a particularly touchy issue in ecumenical discussion, the willingness of the pope to share publicly in a service of worship with non-Catholics set a new pattern and style for subsequent ecumenical activity at the local level. The other event took place on the last working day of the Council, where, simultaneously with a similar service in Istanbul, Pope Paul and Patriarch Athenagoras of the Orthodox Church, mutually lifted the excommunications and anathemas which had technically been in force between the two churches since the eleventh century. This act of mutual pardon was seen as a symbolic step toward the creation of better relationships between the two communions, formally divided since the Great Schism of A.D. 1054.

The above events can be understood within the narrower definition of ecumenism, the relationship of divided Christian bodies toward one another. But there were other events at the Council that had important implications for ecumenism, even if ecumenism was not their direct subject matter. Thus the conciliar decision to affirm the "collegiality of the bishops", who rule over the church in conjunction with the bishop of Rome as head of the episcopal college, was an important step in removing some of the one-sided understanding of papacy that had been formulated by the incompleted agenda of Vatican I, the doctrinal area most divisive in Catholic–non-Catholic relationships. Similarly, the greater recognition of the role of the laity, the strengthening of the understanding of "the priesthood of all believers," the extensive liturgical reforms, and other acts of intramural renewal,

all served to restore a broader stance of "catholicity" or
wholeness in ways that not only brought about self-purifica-
tion, but also brought the church considerably closer to many
of the concerns of Protestantism and Orthodoxy.[6]

In relation to ecumenism as a concern for the plight
of the entire *oikoumene,* it was a document not even on the
original agenda of Vatican II that was probably the most
effective catalyst—the longest single Council document, *The
Church and the World Today.* Commenting on the specifics of
the church in relation to contemporary culture, it deals with
economics, war, atomic weapons, labor unions, conscientious
objection, strikes, and a host of similar problems. That Pope
Paul in the final section of his allocution of September 1963
had specifically encouraged a dialogue with the modern
world, gave essential support for the insistence of many of the
Council fathers that such a document emerge from Vatican II.

Considering where the Catholic Church was when
Paul became pope, and indeed the whole ecumenical climate
of the early 1960's, Paul's ecumenical actions in relation to
Vatican II emerge as very creative ones. Save for the dreary
days at the close of session three, one can convincingly argue
that the ecumenical cause was strongly fostered and greatly
helped by Paul's attitude and leadership. Since the Council,
however, it is impossible not to be struck by a general slowing
down of papal activity in this and other related areas. To the
outside observer it sometimes appears as though the Pope
were almost in a panic, fearful that the Council had become a
kind of Pandora's box, loosing many ills on Catholicism and
the modern world, from which Catholicism, at least, must be
protected by strong rear-guard actions. Thus, although there
are many creative papal actions after December 7, 1965,

---

[6] For a convenient collection of all the conciliar texts, in which the above
and other reforms are elaborated, cf. Abbott and Gallagher, eds., *Documents of Vatican II* (New York: Guild Press, America Press, Association
Press, 1966), 794 pp.

when the council adjourned, there are many others which are bound to create misgivings and even dismay in the hearts of ecumenically-minded Christians, whether Catholics or not. We shall first examine some of the actions that relate directly to the subject-matter of ecumenism.

Positively, the pope has continued to give strong support to the Secretariat for the Promotion of Christian Unity, the official organ through which Roman Catholicism relates to non-Roman Catholic Christian churches.[7] His appointment of Bishop (now Cardinal) Jan Willebrands is a symbol of the depth and integrity of this support, for there are few Roman Catholics in the entire world held in as high esteem by both Protestants and Orthodox as this Dutch theologian, host to all the observers during Vatican II and himself an "observer" at the fourth assembly of the World Council at Uppsala in July 1968. The pope has also given support to the Joint Working Committee of members of the Secretariat and representatives of the World Council of Churches that has had semi-annual meetings since its creation in 1965, discussing such topics as faith and worship, laity, mixed marriages, proselytism, and joint biblical translation.[8] Relations with the Orthodox have continued to develop in the wake of the lifting of the anathemas and excommunications referred to above. There have been three meetings between Pope Paul and the Ecumenical Patriarch Athenagoras, the first in Jerusalem, after which the pope has gone to Istanbul while Athenagoras has come to Rome,[9] and there has been a relaxation of the requirements for Catholic-Orthodox marriages, bringing Latin rite practices into closer conformity with that of the non-Catholic churches of the East.[10] One has the impression, indeed, that it is far easier for Pope Paul to relate to the Eastern

---

[7] Cf. *TPS*, 12, 2: 97–102, 187–189; 13, 4: 320–323; 14, 1: 12–18.

[8] For minutes of the meetings of this group, cf. the files of *The Ecumenical Review*, published quarterly by the World Council of Churches in Geneva.

[9] Cf. *TPS*, 12, 4:342–346.

[10] Cf. *TSP* 12, 2:122–123.

Churches than to those of the West, and that specific steps toward organic reunion are far more likely to be initiated with the former than with the latter.

On a number of matters related to the inner life of Roman Catholicism, Pope Paul's actions have had ecumenical implications. His trips abroad, for example, which have led to his being called *Papa Viaggiante* (the traveling pope), have surely served to dispel some of the inherited imagery of the pope as the prisoner of the Vatican, seeing things only from the miniscule perspective of Vatican City. (It was a big event when, shortly before Vatican II began, Pope John ventured as far outside Rome as the village of Assisi.) Pope Paul's initial trip to Jerusalem, and his subsequent trips to India, to the United Nations, to South America, and to Africa, have served the purpose not only of stimulating Roman Catholic response in those countries, but of opening the papal eyes to a world far removed from the papal palace and neatly manicured gardens behind St. Peter's. On the other hand, the trips have not served, at least yet, to "liberalize" the pope in ways many observers hoped would happen. A trip to India, where overpopulation and starvation are twin miseries, did not lead to a new attitude toward birth control; a trip to South America, where many feel that only radical social change can save a generation from misery and even extinction, became the occasion for a speech designed to moderate and diminish radical politicization; and a trip to Geneva, visiting the World Council of Churches headquarters, was used to reiterate in unmistakable terms the exclusive nature of the Petrine claim to sole headship of the true church.[11]

On the issue of priestly celibacy, the pope has remained adamant against changing the ancient ruling, even though no theological issue, and only a matter of church law, is involved.

[11] The latter speech can also be interpreted as a forthright example of unwillingness to fuzz ecumenical discussion by sentimentality, but even so it can scarcely have helped to thaw the climate between Geneva and Rome.

Consecration to Christ, by virtue of an additional and lofty title like celibacy, evidently gives to the priest, even in the practical field, the maximum efficiency and the best disposition of mind, psychologically and affectively, for the continuous exercise of perfect charity.[12]

The continued imposition of the demand of celibacy has been a major reason for priests leaving the contemporary church, and apparently one of the reasons for a marked drop-off in seminary enrollments. It is thus producing a crisis in the life of Catholicism that will increase as the total number of available priests diminishes.

The attitude toward mixed marriages, e.g., between Roman Catholics and non-Roman Catholics, continues to be a vexing one. *The Instruction on Mixed Marriages,* issued in 1966, though not over the pope's name, can only be appraised as an interim measure, since it granted a few peripheral concessions but did not grapple with fundamental theological issues—e.g., if Protestants are already part of the church, however imperfectly, by virtue of baptism, then a special situation is created in a Catholic-Protestant marriage in which the degree of commonly-shared faith should make a creative contribution, rather than being a stumbling block, to such a marriage. Although the matter was further discussed at the first meeting of the Synod of Bishops in the fall of 1967, little progress was made. In local situations, the disparity between possibilities open to the Catholic and the Protestant partners in a marriage ceremony is still a great ecumenical irritant.

Many actions in the field of liturgical reform have had ecumenical overtones. The thrust of the conciliar constitution *On the Sacred Liturgy* was ecumenically creative, since it increased lay participation, introduced the vernacular, put more stress on Scripture and sermon, and in various

---

[12] *Sacerdotalis Caelibatus.* Cf. *TPS,* 12, 3, for the full text.

other ways served to show how much Catholics and non-Catholics share liturgically. But as experimentation began to take place in Catholic parishes, the boom began to be lowered from Rome, and an attitude of impeding initiative appeared as the dominant one.

In January 1967, Pope Paul urged moderation concerning liturgical innovations in general: all change must come through the bishops, there must be no startling eccentricities, "liturgical changes ought to be introduced gradually," and so on.[13] The following April, addressing the Commission for Implementing the Constitution of the Sacred Liturgy, the pope warned against "illegitimate liturgical innovations," which "frequently are shaped to suit individual whims and often take forms that are wholly at odds with the precepts now in force in the Church. This greatly upsets many upright Church members." [14]

In an address to the Secretariat for Christian Unity in November 1968, Pope Paul spoke of "rash ecumenical gestures," and thinking particularly of occasional instances of intercommunion, went on to say:

> In these gestures, it seems we find a desire to prod the slow pace of what some have called "institutional ecumenism." In them we find an impatient anxiety to implement ecumenism in deeds, without any further delay, through gestures that are felt to be, or are supposed to be, "prophetic." In them we see an excessive haste in the process of rapprochement; it does not wait for the necessary maturation of doctrine that must precede practical action—trying, as it were, to somehow force the hand of the responsible authorities in the different denominations involved.[15]

[13] Cf. *TPS* 12, 1: 12.
[14] Cf. *TPS* 12, 2: 112. One wonders if an even better colloquial translation could not be achieved by rendering the third word from the end as "uptight."
[15] Cf. *TPS,* 13, 4: 322.

And although the pope goes on to say that "this impatience sometimes has a positive aspect," and can be done for good motives, "as soon as it calls into question the institution created by Christ to serve the Christian people, one can only agree with the sentiment once expressed by St. Paul regarding his brothers in Israel: 'I bear them witness that they have zeal for God, but a zeal that is unenlightened.' " [16]

While it is clear that some liturgical innovations have indeed gotten out of bounds, it is also clear that some of the most creative attempts to relate Catholic faith to the contemporary world have come through liturgical innovation, and that priests or congregations moving in this direction have increasingly felt, not the support, but the censure of Rome.

In the area of theological reflection a similar caution has become the hallmark of papal reactions. Almost on the eve of the fourth assembly of the World Council of Churches, Pope Paul issued his *Credo,* an attempt to state the Catholic faith in terms that would speak to the modern world.[17] But the affirmation involved little more than a running commentary on the Apostles' and Nicene creeds, augmented by reference to later items of defined Roman Catholic dogma. While it was seen as a competent statement of traditional Catholic faith, few commentators felt that the *Credo* offered any help in relating that faith to the modern world, and one Catholic went so far as to describe it as "a bold step into the fourteenth century."

Increasing numbers of papal speeches have warned against theological innovation, and although individuals have not been mentioned, there has been fairly clear indication that the Dutch in particular have caused papal unease.[18] Indeed, the Congregation of Sacred Doctrine (replacing the old Holy

---

[16] *Ibid.*

[17] The full text is in *TPS* 13, 3: 273–282.

[18] This concern dates back at least to *Mysterium Fidei,* an encyclical issued during the Council, reiterating traditional views of the Real Presence against views gaining currency among Dutch theologians.

Office), which was supposed to foster theological discussion
and investigation, has issued various warnings about the im-
propriety of too much theological discussion and investigation, and matters became so tense that, when proceedings
were to be initiated against Edward Schillebeeckx of Nijme-
gen, and Hans Küng of Tubingen, a group of Catholic theologians issued a statement in November 1968 from Zurich, in-
sisting that "the freedom of theologians and theology in the
service of the Church, regained by Vatican II, must not now
be jeopardized again." It was their conviction that subtle
forms of inquisitorial technique were being reintroduced and
that orderly procedures, safeguarding freedom of thought and
inquiry, were on the block. In addition to Küng and Schillebeeckx, such theologians as Yves Congar, Karl Rahner, Ro-
land Murphy, and Dominic-Marie Chenu signed the protest.

It may be objected that such activities by the Congregation of Sacred Doctrine are not, strictly speaking,
"papal activities," but it is clear that such activities, if not initiated by the pope, proceed at least with his tacit consent, and
that, when one is speaking of papacy and Vatican, no neat
lines of division can finally be drawn. A similar situation ob-
tains in relation to the papacy and the Synod of Bishops. An
initial meeting of the Synod was held in October 1967, where
a variety of topics was discussed, but the Synod was without
power to initiate its own agenda or to take any action other
than advisory to the pope. This meant that many burning issues, such as birth control and clerical celibacy, were ex-
cluded from discussion, and the pope was thus deprived of the
advice of his fellow bishops on matters that have subsequently
been of increasing distress to him. Unless the powers of the
Synod are increased, the much-vaunted principle of "collegiality," enacted at Vatican II, will remain *de facto* a dead letter.

In surveying papal actions since the Council that
are either substantively concerned with ecumenical relations
between the churches or are intramural Catholic issues with
theological implications for other churches, it is clear that

Pope Paul has followed an increasingly cautious path. At its best, his policy can be interpreted as an endeavor to ensure that the church is not torn apart by schism, and as a way of emphasizing that it is his duty to be pope to all Catholics, and not just to progressive ones. In less favorable terms, the policy can be faulted for having stifled much creative initiative within the church and having forced considerable numbers of responsible Catholics, both priests and nuns, to despair of significant reform within the institutional framework of the present church.

On the other hand, when Pope Paul has dealt with the theme of "the church and the world," he has been at the forefront of leadership within the church (bracketing for the moment the issue of birth control, to which attention will presently be directed). If Pope Paul has appeared to slow down intramural change in Roman Catholicism, he has appeared to hasten the development of Catholic sensitivity on matters that concern the whole family of man.

On the issue of Vietnam, for example, Pope Paul has been far ahead of virtually all the American bishops. While increasing numbers of American clergy, both Protestant and Jewish, were protesting the war and the immorality of America's presence in Vietnam, the American hierarchy refused to engage in criticism of the Johnson-Humphrey-Rusk line that was finally repudiated by the American people long before it was repudiated by the American bishops. But back in 1966, in the encyclical *Christi Matrii Rosarii,* Pope Paul was inveighing against the war. At a time when "negotiating" with the enemy was unthinkable to the State Department and the White House, and when military escalation was the American response to peace feelers, the pope wrote:

> Once again We raise Our voice "with a loud cry and with tears," urgently beseeching those who rule over nations to do everything they can to see to

it that the conflagration spreads no farther but
rather is completely extinguished. . . . Let all
those responsible bring about the necessary conditions for the laying down of arms before the possibility of doing so is taken away by the pressure of
events. Those in whose hands rests the safety of
the human race should realize that in this day and
age they have a very grave obligation in conscience. . . . In the name of the Lord We cry out
to them to stop. Men must come together and get
down to sincere negotiations. Things must be settled now, even at the cost of some loss or inconvenience, for later they may have to be settled at
the cost of immense harm and enormous slaughter
that cannot even be imagined now.[19]

One can scarcely imagine how the course of American history might have been changed if even a dozen members
of the American hierachy had been willing in 1966 to be as
forthright as their pope.

Another example of papal leadership in the field of
"secular ecumenism" is the important encyclical *Populorum
Progressio* (On the Development of Peoples).[20] In this encyclical Pope Paul addresses not only Catholics but likewise "all
men of goodwill," urging them to responsible involvement for
the economic well-being of the world's poor, in terms radical
enough to be characterized by the *Wall Street Journal* as
"warmed-over Marxism." The document is important not only
in its own right but also because it was one of the documents
used in preparation for the Beirut Conference on World Development in April 1968, and for the fourth world assembly of
the World Council of Churches in Uppsala in July 1968. Pope
Paul had earlier given approval for the creation of a Papal
Commission for Studies on Justice and Peace in January

[19] Cf. *TPS*, 11, 3:222–223.
[20] Cf. *TPS*, 12, 2: 144–172. The encyclical was issued on Easter Sunday.

1967,[21] to implement Catholic concern for world economic development, and growing out of the impetus of Beirut and Uppsala this became an ecumenically-oriented commission comprising members not only from the Vatican but also from the World Council, known as the Commission for Society, Development and Peace (SODEPAX), with headquarters in Geneva, but headed by a Catholic priest, George Dunne, S.J. Thus in the realm of practical concern for the world's starving and despairing, there has been papal initiative and involvement leading to an ecumenical structure that can begin to coordinate the concern and the resources of both the Vatican and the World Council.[22]

It would be a happy occasion if one could conclude at this point, but there is a further papal action, full of ecumenical import, to which attention must be given in conclusion. This is the encyclical *Humanae Vitae,* issued on July 29, 1968. Since other essays in this volume deal with the substance of the encyclical, the following comments are limited to its ecumenical implications.[23]

If any issue is "ecumenical" in the sense that it concerns the whole of "the inhabited world," birth control is such an issue. It is increasingly clear that unless a way is found to curb population increases, there will be massive world starvation perhaps within a decade. Certain demographers already feel that it is too late to save many parts of the world from devastating and destructive hunger and lingering death. The "rhythm method" of birth control is simply not reliable enough to achieve this end, even if its subtleties could be grasped by

[21] Cf. *TPS,* 12, 2: 103–106.

[22] Cf. also the appraisal of an earlier papal "social encyclical," contained in Paul's address, *"Rerum Novarum" Today,* given in May 1966, *TPS,* 11, 3: 324–329.

[23] Further documentation for the conclusions briefly set forth here can be found in *The Ecumenical Revolution,* revised and expanded edition, Ch. 17, *"Humanae Vitae* and the Crisis of Authority," pp. 327–347, and in my contribution to Curran, ed., *Contraception: Authority and Dissent* (New York: Herder and Herder, 1969), pp. 193–215.

illiterate peasants. Some form of "artificial" limitation of births is clearly a sociological necessity. Thus, as the New York *Times* editorialized on the day after the encyclical appeared, "When the Church presumes to speak for one-sixth of mankind, on an issue that could affect the very survival of the human race, others cannot remain indifferent."

Thus the encyclical's impact on the non-Catholic world, forbidding all "artificial" means of preventing birth, is a devastating one. The encyclical appears to compound what many consider the number one problem facing mankind, the geometrically-increasing birth rate, and to hasten the day when the human race may suffer in a fashion unparalleled in human history. The impact of the encyclical on Protestant-Catholic relations has also been grave. For some time birth control has been a matter on which Protestant and Catholic teaching has been divergent, and the attempt to impose Catholic practice on couples in "mixed marriages" has been a source of great ecumenical as well as psychological tension. The attempt to base the teaching against contraception on "natural law," which therefore can be held to be binding on all men whether Catholics or not, has exacerbated the problem of the relation of church and state. Furthermore, the issue of birth control raises that area of theology most difficult for non-Catholics, the issue of papal authority. On a matter where informed Protestants simply believe the pope is wrong, the image of his authority is hardly enhanced when, after years of study, he reiterates more emphatically than ever before the old position.

But perhaps the greatest difficulties with the encyclical have been posed for Roman Catholics themselves. The papal encyclical appeared to be noncollegial since, although three papal commissions suggested a change in teaching, the pope ignored their advice and acted unilaterally. The encyclical appeared theologically suspect, since it offered no new arguments for the position, repeating only old arguments that had been challenged in Catholic journals and books for several years. And the encyclical went against what had *de facto* become the practice of countless Catholic couples, who, when told in the confessional that the teaching of the church was in a state of doubt, followed the traditional Catholic practice of consulting their own consciences. Having used contraceptives for long periods of time, as a result, and having found that their marriages were not only not jeopardized but actually strengthened by the freedom of "conjugal love" thereby made possible, they were not about to be persuaded by the encyclical that contraceptives would, as the pope declared in the encyclical, make the man look upon the woman as a mere instrument for his gratification, or destroy the fabric of the family. Protest against the encyclical was therefore particularly strong within the Catholic Church, and not only married couples but hundreds of priests and theologians rallied around the notion that the encyclical need not be binding on couples acting in good conscience, later followed in this judgment by many national bishops' conferences.

For all the above reasons, it might seem that *Humanae Vitae* is nothing short of an ecumenical catastrophe. However, the unintended by-product of *Humanae Vitae* may in fact be ecumenically creative. For up until its issuance, papal authority was the chief stumbling block between Protestants and Catholics, and at the end of the day of dialogue probably the only remaining stumbling block. There has always been a lurking Protestant fear that when the last ecumenical exchange had been held, Protestants would still be expected to give some kind of unyielding and even unthinking obedience to whatever the pope said. But with one stroke of the pen, Pope Paul undid that entire bit of imagery. For the Catholic reaction to the encyclical has made perfectly clear that Catholics who in good conscience disagree with the encyclical can go on disagreeing with it in good conscience and remain good Catholics. Events since its issuance have established that those who live in communion with the See of Rome make up their minds not simply by waiting for the pope to speak, but by assessing a number of factors, such as a careful evaluation of the facts, prayer, reflection on what theologians say and what bishops say, reflection on what the bishop of Rome says, examination of their own consciences, out of which amalgam of events they come to a decision which may or may not be in accord with the position taken by the bishop of Rome. Surely a Protestant is willing to engage in a similar exercise, and to take seriously the convictions of similar authorities. If this is, in fact, what the authority of the pope is going to mean in the future, then the biggest stumbling block of all is no longer unsurmountable.

It is an irony that Pope Paul, who has made so many creative contributions to the cause of world development and peace, will probably be remembered longest in history for *Humanae Vitae*. But the fact that even out of it, quite undesignedly, some further ecumenical breakthroughs may come, is an example of an overruling divine irony, and of the power of the Holy Spirit to make creative use of whatsoever men may offer up to Him.

The Style
of Paul's Leadership

Gary MacEoin

Mr. MacEoin is a newsman, lawyer, linguist, and
author of a dozen books. He reported on the
Second Vatican Council and on the Synod of
Bishops in 1967 and 1969 for publications both
secular and religious in Europe, Asia, Africa,
North and South America.
He is author of a book on the Council and
coauthor of a book on the 1967 Synod. He writes
a weekly syndicated column on world affairs,
which specializes in religious matters and
problems of development in the Third World.
He is currently engaged in three writing projects:
a book on Latin America (his third); a study of
the theology of the laity; and a further segment
of his personal memoirs.

"If you haven't made up your mind about Pope Paul, I have," an archbishop said to me in Rome during the final session of the Council in 1965. "And I'll tell you what I think. I think that if Paul had followed Pius XII without the intervening presence of John XXIII, nobody would have known that one pope had died and another been elected."

The speaker was a man in his seventies, a brilliant mind, a very traditionalist theologian, with close personal ties to the reactionary curialist bloc in the Curia. In Pius XII's time, he had suffered grievously and unjustly from curial incompetence, ineptitude, and politicking with the civil authority in his homeland. He was intellectually comfortable with the old ideas, but his existential condition as a pastor rejected the possibility of returning to the pre-Council situation. And he was disturbed because he realized that Paul, lacking pastoral exposure and feedback in contemporary life situations, felt no such pressure to change.

Four years and two meetings of the Synod of Bishops later, the archbishop's analysis still holds up. It is doubtful if the church ever before moved so fast as it has since Paul became pope. The Council he had inherited after its first session continued through three more sessions, and he promulgated the many revolutionary documents it produced. The Synod of Bishops was created, and by its second meeting it was guaranteed some significant control over itself. The principle of collegiality, unheard of ten years earlier, had become common currency and started to find practical expression. Thanks to the church's new understanding of religious freedom, of ecumenical relations, and of its function in the world, a pope could travel in peace and respect in every continent.

But could Paul take credit for these advances, or did he even see them as such? I do not think so. At almost every point he appears as an unhappy assentor to changes for which he sees no need and feels no enthusiasm. His concept of ruling is to keep things from changing. His vision is a rule of persons rather than a rule of law. He does not understand the need for intermediate structures, still less for grassroots structures which enable the ruled to create social units to defend themselves and express their views. What he wants is an unstructured proletariat, literally a flock of sheep. *Divide et impera* (divide and rule) was a maxim of Imperial Rome, one of many perpetuated in the practice of papal Rome.

Whether he likes it or not, Pope Paul is going to be judged primarily on his contribution to the Council and to the Synod of Bishops which grew from it. These are the central events of his term of office to date, and the likelihood of their being eclipsed by something more noteworthy is remote to the point of practical exclusion. The Council and Synod provide ample material to permit evaluation of the nature and quality of his leadership. The evidence they furnish falls short of eliminating all ambiguities and internal contradictions. I think, nevertheless, that it is sufficient for the construction of a substantially accurate and complete portrait.

I believe, to start, that several major conclusions can be drawn from the Council and Synod experience. One is that Paul will accept and implement a course of action, no matter how repugnant to him personally, provided the bishops of the world express a clear consensus and insist on action. Another is that, whenever such consensus is lacking, he will not commit himself but will tend in his temporizing to favor the conservative side. Yet another is that, when the bishops force a course of action on him, he will surround his compliance with a hedge of verbal reservations designed to leave the way open to backtrack later. This hedging is simply at a juridical level, ignoring the realities of power and the existential requirements of the situations.

The classic example of Paul's technique is the *Nota Praevia* attached to the Constitution on the Church of Vatican II. Its purpose was to spell out in juridical language, and from the viewpoint of the papacy as it had understood itself since Vatican Council I, the limited meaning to be assigned to the affirmation by the Fathers of the collegial character of church government. The Council in the document had already been quite specific in its formulation of papal rights and prerogatives. "The Roman Pontiff," it said, "has full, supreme and universal power. . . . He can always exercise this power freely. . . . Together with its head, the Roman Pontiff, and never without this head, the episcopal order is the subject of supreme and full power over the universal church. But this power can be exercised only with the consent of the Roman Pontiff. . . ." Objectively evaluated, the *Nota Praevia* does not go any further. As Avery Dulles says in a note to the Abbott-Gallagher translation of *The Documents of Vatican II,* "all commentators agree that this Note does not weaken or modify the teaching" of the Fathers. What it does is to reformulate in petulant and defensively aggressive terms what the Fathers had already proclaimed as lying outside the issue. Paul did not like what the Fathers insisted on doing. He bowed to their insistence. While bowing, he reasserted his disapproval.

The creation of the Synod offers another excellent example of the technique. By the third session of the Council, a clear consensus had developed in favor of the establishment of a small body representative of the world's bishops to form with the pope a permanent policy-making and decision-making body. Paul publicly acknowledged this consensus and agreed to implement it. A few months later, he expanded the College of Cardinals by adding a considerable number of diocesan bishops. The word was passed by "informed sources close to the Vatican" that this was the pope's way of fulfilling his commitment.

Such may well have been his intention. But the reaction of the bishops was so overwhelmingly negative that another announcement followed quickly. There was to be a new body to be known as the Synod of Bishops. It would have two main forms, an ordinary and an extraordinary Synod. Most of the members of both bodies would be elected by their fellow bishops. The real reason for the two types was not, and still is not, very clear. The extraordinary would tend to be somewhat less representative and rather more conservative. Perhaps it was hoped that it would be more likely to go along with the pope on a sticky issue.

What was most obvious about both kinds of Synod was the gap between what the bishops wanted and what they got. At every point, the stress was on the pope's total discretionary power. He could call a meeting when he so decided. He alone controlled the agenda. He was free to accept or reject the Synod's advice. Juridically, he gave absolutely nothing. In political terms, nevertheless, he had given quite a lot, perhaps more than he realized, as had become evident by the end of the second Synod session.

Paul's readiness to bow to a consensus was illustrated by the most important action taken by the 1967 Synod, its rejection of the Curia's viewpoint on freedom of discussion in the church.

Freedom of theological discussion has been the most bitter internal issue in the Catholic Church for two centuries, since the Age of the Enlightenment. From the French Revolution right up to Vatican Council II, the Holy Office blocked every attempt to come to honest terms with the explosion of secular knowledge. It insisted, first of all, on a monolithic front. Nobody on the Catholic side could make any concession without its prior approval. And, next, when it had to yield, it yielded minimally, reluctantly, and in ambiguous terms that sought to reaffirm continuity while introducing change. The consequence was a steady widening of the gap between what theologians and other educated Catholics believed and what "the church" taught on evolution, on demythologization of the Bible, on the meaning of conciliar definitions, on authority in the church, on the meaning of the eucharistic presence of Christ.

When Pope John called the Council, Cardinal Ottaviani, head of the Holy Office, suspected that a few hothead bishops might want to use this assembly to challenge his monopoly. Wishing to anticipate trouble, he prepared draft documents on revelation, the moral order (dangers of subjectivism, abuse of psychoanalytic techniques, and so forth), and the deposit of faith (pantheism, existentialism, modernism, the family, and chastity). The Council at its first session quickly rejected all of these documents as irrelevant and harmful, too scholastic, too juridical, too canonical, too centered on morality, not biblical enough.

Ottaviani and his associates wouldn't take no for an answer. In July 1966, seven months after the Council ended, they requested all bishops and heads of religious orders to check off on a list the errors most threatening in their respective countries or religious families. The list covered the same ground as his rejected documents, and he hoped it would produce a survey of world conditions threatening enough to warrant an encyclical worthy to rank with Pius IX's *Syllabus of Errors*.

The bishops, however, refused the bait a second time. The "secret" project was leaked to the press and thus submitted to a public analysis which led to a worldwide negative evaluation. Many national hierarchies in Europe and

America replied either that no significant errors troubled them or that condemnation was no longer the way to combat error. A more basic criticism came from Africa and Asia. Many bishops said their preoccupations were not those of the Holy Office but rather the task of relating the church to a world in rapid change. They also said that the formulation of various issues, such as that of the eucharistic presence and the virginity of Mary, reflected a Western mentality foreign to their ways of thought. Nothing is more obvious than the need to express the life and message of Christianity in forms meaningful to the non-Western cultures of the world, but the Roman mind is dead set against a step which would inevitably lead to ecclesiastical decolonization.

In spite of two reverses, the Holy Office refused to accept defeat. The key item on the agenda of the first Synod of Bishops (1967) asked the bishops to advise the pope on how he should deal with current "dangers to the faith." The position paper on the item was prepared in Cardinal Ottaviani's curial department, the Congregation for the Doctrine of the Faith, the ex-Holy Office. Learning from bitter experience, its authors prepared a very sophisticated package. When it was opened, however, the contents were the same as before.

Already before the start of the Synod, Melchite Archbishop Neophyte Edelby publicly criticized the project in a lecture given in Rome. "The church currently needs greater freedom rather than greater repression," he declared. "We therefore wish the coming Synod of Bishops to say no more on doctrinal matters than the Council said. Neither would I like it to undertake interpretation of the Council's doctrinal affirmations. It has neither the competence nor the grace. . . . The Synod should reassert confidence in the Holy Spirit, encouraging pluriformity as against the recent tradition of absolute uniformity, including dogmatic theology, theological methodology, biblical research, and patristic tradition. The Synod's doctrinal task is to create mutual confidence in the church, to favor freedom of expression, while interesting the greatest possible number of people in the life of theology."

The debate quickly confirmed a consensus of the bishops in favor of the Edelby thesis. "Truth can never be imposed like a law," Cardinal Paul Emile Léger affirmed. "It is a mystery into which we must search. In this respect, the document is not in agreement with Vatican Council II. Its main defect is that it confuses errors with inadequacies of formulation of the truth. . . . Of course, there are difficult questions in the church, but the basic question is what is the truth and what is the mystery still to be explored. It is not by a document of this kind but by an exploration conducted by the entire church, with all its trends and at all its different levels, that we can hope to resolve the crisis." To which Cardinal Bernard Jan Alfrink added: "It would be appropriate to draft a document to express thanks to the theologians. That would be more useful than to draw up a catalogue of errors or even a list of the truths of faith."

The next step was to decide what to do about the substantive issue, that is to say, what advice to offer the pope. The Rules of Procedure (Article 34, paragraph 1) authorize the President of the Synod, *with the pope's permission and according to rules set up by him,* to create a study commission to examine a disputed matter further. For the first and only time at the session, this section was invoked, and it is proper to note that Pope Paul applied it in such a way as to give full expression to what was already the clear will of the Synod Fathers. He agreed to the creation of a commission, directing the Synod to elect eight members while he himself would name four more. The Synod chose an essentially progressive group. It included Archbishop Edelby, Cardinal Leo Josef Suenens and Cardinal Julius Döpfner, the most conservative choices being Bishops (later Cardinals) Carlo Colombo and John Wright, both generally rated at the Council as ahead of center, although subsequently negative in their response to concrete efforts at updating the church.

The pope's nominees were even more surprising.

When similar elections had taken place at the Council, both Pope John and Pope Paul eased the sting of defeat for the minority by naming some of its members. Now, instead, Pope Paul selected spokesmen for the emerging cultures of Latin America, Africa, and Asia. In addition, he confirmed the decision of the bishops by appointing as chairman the bishop to whom they had given most votes, Cardinal Franjo Seper of Yugoslavia. Cardinal Seper's views were already clearly on the record. "Christians who defend the established order and the unchangeableness of social structures too stubbornly," he had said in a Council intervention, "are partly responsible for modern atheism."

The report of the Seper commission, overwhelmingly approved by the Synod over the opposition of the Ottaviani bloc, gave the green light to a continuance of free discussion in the church. It agreed that "unwarranted innovations, false opinions and even errors in the faith" have appeared as a result of the efforts to implement the call of Pope John and of Vatican Council II to reformulate the truth in terms meaningful to contemporary man. It insisted, however, that these problems could not be explained or resolved by blaming the theologians or criticizing the failure of the magisterium to act. Rather, they flow from the nature of modern civilization and the forward movement of culture, in "man's ever-increasing awareness of the evolution of the universe and of his own life and history." Concretely, the task of preaching the faith in the context of the specific advances in all fields of knowledge "belongs first of all to the bishops, with their helpers in the priesthood, aided by members of religious orders. But it also belongs to laymen engaged in teaching the faith and in catechizing; it belongs, in fact, to all the faithful, and in a special way to parents in regard to their children. All the children of the church, therefore, each according to the charism given him, must be aware of their responsibility for passing on the holy gift of faith to the men of our time."

The Synod had spoken unambiguously. Its func-

tion, however, was purely advisory. How would the pope respond? The answer came, in a manner that was typically
Roman in its symbolism if un-Roman in its apparent finality.
Ten weeks after the Synod ended, the pope accepted Cardinal
Ottaviani's resignation and named to replace him the man the
bishops had chosen as their spokesman against Ottaviani, Cardinal Seper. It was a striking expression of acceptance of the
episcopal will.

In subsequent months, nevertheless, it emerged that
the change was more Roman and less final than it seemed at
first. Ottaviani was made pro-prefect emeritus and continued
to take an active part in the affairs of the Congregation. Whenever Seper was away from his desk, Ottaviani took possession
of it and made decisions on his own authority, creating the
most extraordinary two-headed monstrosity since Janus. The
schizophrenic control continues at the time of this writing.

The 1967 Synod also offered several illustrations of
the correctness of the thesis that where consensus is lacking
Paul will avoid a firm ruling, while tending to favor the conservative side in his temporizing. The two best examples were
the agenda items on mixed marriages and on liturgical experimentation.

The Synod fathers seem to have agreed in principle that the March 1965 instruction on mixed marriages
fell short of implementing the wishes of Vatican Council II.
They saw the validity of the criticism of a spokesman for the
World Council of Churches who described it as far less than
"what could be expected after the promulgation of the Declaration on Religious Freedom, the Decree on Ecumenism, and
particularly the discussion of the problem of mixed marriages
at the Vatican Council." In the debate, however, they failed
to find any substantial common ground. Changes which one
bishop saw as helpful in his particular pastoral situation were
invariably challenged by another bishop as harmful in his.
The end result was a recommendation that existing legislation
should remain substantially unchanged, the most significant of

the minor changes proposed being that the bishops themselves be granted more dispensatory discretion.

The item on liturgy produced a similar reaction. Two contradictory concepts dominated the thinking. Recognizing that the liturgical changes introduced since the Council had served mainly to reveal the underlying inappropriateness of the Roman liturgy as a meaningful form of worship for many modern Christians, the bishops wanted to continue to search for something better. Many were simultaneously obsessed with a fear of the kind of free experimentation that had become contagiously popular in the Underground Church in various countries. Their anxiety to maintain uniformity in the preconciliar sense was evident, and they were willing to reaffirm strict control by the Congregation of Rites, if this was necessary for that purpose. Some even indicated a desire to reach quickly a new type of liturgy that would be as inflexible as was the liturgy before the Council, ignoring the Council's own concept of a church committed to progressive change as the sole constant in our evolving world.

Understandably enough, Pope Paul avoided a decisive stand on the issues on which the Synod fathers vacillated. He did, however, take various steps which concretely favored the conservatives. One was to reject the request of the United States bishops to set up centers for liturgical experimentation in some universities, and to give the bishops' conference authority to permit a bishop to conduct experiments in his own diocese. Another was the naming of the moderate conservative Cardinal Benno Gut to head both the Congregation of Rites and the Council for Liturgical Reform. Subsequently, there came a curiously ambiguous announcement which seemed to proclaim the end of the period of experimentation without quite doing so.

From one point of view, the rejection of the request of the United States' bishops was not so strange. In an interview given in February 1968, shortly before his death, Archbishop Paul Hallinan said that most of the United States' bish-

ops were against further changing of the liturgy, and that it
had taken him six hours on the podium at their November
1967 meeting to persuade them to go along with his proposal
to ask Rome's permission to experiment. From another point
of view, it was a very remarkable decision. Shortly before the
1967 Synod, the bishops of Canada notified Rome that they
had authorized all their members to conduct such liturgical
experiments as they judged proper in their respective dioceses,
and Rome sent back a letter congratulating them on their apostolic initiative. What the United States asked and was refused
was much more modest than what Canada was praised for
doing.

The 1969 "extraordinary" Synod revealed no
change in the style of Paul's leadership. All the preparations
were made behind the velvet curtain of curial secrecy, and as
they gradually emerged to the light of twentieth-century day,
they revealed the intrigue, maneuvering, and deception which
characterize the Curia's concepts of church government. The
secret working paper circulated for comments by bishops
inevitably became public, and its contents brought a chill to
everyone committed to the directions given by Vatican II. It
established a concerted effort by the Curia to return to the
days of Pius XII.

The plan backfired, thanks to the courage of Cardinal Suenens. Correctly judging the decisive power of public
opinion, he formulated a program of institutional reforms
which quickly won overwhelming support. He called for regular meetings of the Synod in "ordinary" session, control by the
Synod over its agenda, a permanent secretariat independent of
the Curia, election of popes by the Synod, changes in the
method of naming bishops to end the curial monopoly, and a
reshaping of the functions and responsibilities of nuncios in
order to establish collegial control over them.

This show of force brought a quick retreat. The
opening statement to the Synod by Cardinal Seper reformu-
lated the working paper in terms which Cardinal Suenens and

his supporters found acceptable as a basis for discussion. By the end of the meeting, they had made significant progress. Paul had agreed to hold an "ordinary" Synod every two years. The Synod's permanent secretariat would be strengthened. The bishops would be given a voice in the agenda. Other proposals made by the Synod would receive serious and sympathetic consideration.

It was a major advance. But it must be noted again that it was forced, and that everything was formulated in terms that left open the way to return to the past. It was in fact the now typical stand-off. What it ensured was that the energies of the church would be dissipated for at least the next two years until the following Synod in disputes over housekeeping frivolities. The church's substantive mission to mankind would have to continue to take second place.

To what extent Pope Paul himself agrees with all of this is a question that probably has little meaning. What I think is important is to understand the extent to which he is trapped in a system that effectively leaves him no freedom of decision. Otherwise, one may be tempted to hope that a change of persons, the introduction of outsiders into the Curia, for example, is all that is needed. Cardinal Suenens is under no such illusion. He will settle for nothing less than a change of structures.

Most people live quite comfortably in the environment to which they are accustomed. They accept their own experience as normal. Pope Paul shows no indication of being an exception to this rule. It takes a man of Pope John's stature to recognize (and admit) that he is "in a sack." Those who are unhappy with the situation tend to agree that, given Paul's somewhat hesitant and diffident temperament, he could not do more than he does. "It is interesting that very few people blame the pope, personally," Rosemary Haughton observed recently in a context similar to that discussed here. I recall a remark made to me by a peritus during the final Council session, during one of those black moments when it seemed that the whole church might blow apart. The issue was family planning, and the intransigents were trying to get the fathers to reaffirm Pius XII's condemnation of contraception. "You cannot possibly imagine the pressures to which Pope Paul is being subjected," he said. "Any ordinary man would break under them." Similar praise of the pope was voiced several times during the 1969 Synod by German theologian Bernard Häring, an outspoken critic of the system. Paul's entire attitude during the Synod, where he attended the meetings and heard more outspoken criticism than any pope of modern times, was described by Father Häring as showing how successful he had been in overcoming his temperamental hesitancy and distrust.

The sunny skies which smiled on Rome during the first half of October 1969 may indeed have had an impact on the pope's temperamental hesitancy and distrust. They did not, however, change the basic pattern of his thought or persuade him to reformulate the issues positively. When the first Synod two years earlier asked for the creation of an International Commission of Theologians to represent and express the many currents of theology within the contemporary church, it urged confidence, freedom of expression, an open exploration of mystery and search for truth. When Paul addressed the inaugural meeting of that body just before the second session of the Synod, his appeal to it was "to defend the people of God from the numerous, excessive, and pressing errors that are assailing the divine deposit of truth."

But, I repeat, Paul's private opinions are at best of marginal significance. He operates on the—correct—assumption that the system makes the decisions. And few know better than he what that means. He had a ringside seat during Pius XII's long, unsuccessful struggle to bypass the Curia in his dealings with the universal church. Nor can it be assumed that his sympathies were with Pius. His total training and experience were within the single framework of the Roman ecclesiastical system, from the time he entered the

Gregorian University in 1920 through the Academy of Noble Ecclesiastics and the Secretariat of State, right up to his ap-appointment to the archbishopric of Milan in 1954. In addition, apart from five months in Poland in 1923, his service was entirely within the confines of the Vatican itself. He was, in consequence, always accustomed to authoritarian officials who made their decisions on the basis of their personal judgment of the power factors involved. The administrative procedures practiced in the church, though (in Cardinal Felici's felicitous understatement) "somewhat deficient," are the ones with which he has always lived. It is consequently understandable that, when speaking of change in the Curia, he should insist that it be slow and partial "because of the respect which the persons and traditions merit." The principle, nevertheless, is significantly different from that laid down by St. Paul for the use of authority in II Corinthians 13:7, namely, that there should be a primacy of the objective good of the believers even at the price of possible loss of prestige to the ruler of the community.

Every evaluation of Pope Paul's style of using power must start from a recognition of this training and lifelong experience, extremely intensive but extremely narrow. There is a real glimpse of this thinking in a brief passage in his address to the first working session of the 1967 Synod, in which he referred to the "scholars and publicists eager to analyse the juridical aspects of this institution and to determine, as far as they can, its form and function." Far from encouraging such laudable interest in the changing church, he dismissed them as one would people impelled by curiosity to stick their noses in what was none of their business. This concept of a rule of persons rather than of a rule of law, to which I referred earlier, comes through in all his approaches to reform of the Curia. Replying to the repeated requests from Vatican Council II for such reform, he insisted that some technical changes were desirable and would be gradually introduced, but that there was no great need for structural reforms. And even the much-

touted updating of the Curia in August 1967, shortly before
the first Synod convened, was confined to the technical area.
According to Father Edward D. Vogt, of the University of
Bergen (Norway), a specialist in the sociology of bureaucracy,
it stripped away the façade in order to reveal the real but previously unacknowledged mechanisms of decision. It seemed
"to give legitimation to the present oligarchical rule of inner-
circle cardinals," and "to come dangerously close to the reduction of the pope to a figure-head constitutional monarch,
with the Cardinal Secretary of State as the head of his government, ruling in his majesty's name."

        An even more intimate glimpse into Paul's mind is
available in *The Pope Speaks: Dialogues of Paul VI with
Jean Guitton* (New York, Meredith Press, 1968). Here we
find a sensitive, spiritual, intellectual man, whose contact with
life is mediated through books, and whose range of reading
and consequently range of concern are those of a student in a
traditional Catholic seminary of the 1920s. It is a world in
which experience is minimal and therefore suspect. It is a
static world of unchanging categories. Typical reflections are:
"May I remind you of the teaching of the church from the beginning, which is essential, invariable . . . ?" "They corre-
spond to a design that is invariable although circumstances
change." "Fifteen centuries have passed, a brief interval."

        For us who live in the accelerated and foreshort-
ened time-space continuum of the twentieth century, it is very
difficult to comprehend the mentality that sees fifteen hundred
years as a brief interval and that is consequently ready to
allow a further fifteen hundred for the introduction of changes
that we feel cannot delay fifteen without building up explosive
tensions.

        When I was last in Rome in October 1969, I went
into the Vatican one day, past the fancy-dress boy soldiers, to
visit the Camposanto, once the site of Nero's Circus, just behind the Palace of the Holy Office. It is a combination monas-
tery-cemetery. One enters through an opening in a fortress

wall to the monastery garden which is also the cemetery. One walks on top of graves twenty feet deep. When the coffins pile up to the surface, the lower ones are removed and the crumbled bones are relocated in urns in the monastery's walls.

Here I met a grave monsignore with chiseled features. He had spent a lifetime of prayer and study in this stylized yesterday, listening year after year to the ghosts of the martyrs sighing in the nerve-irritating sirocco and the rheumaticky *tramontana*. He spoke to me about an enormous collection of commentaries of the Fathers on the Scriptures, on which he is working. Graciously he tried to explain it to me, his didactic technique quickly revealing that he assumed me to be as ignorant of his world as he apparently was of mine. He talked down to me, as priests were long taught to talk down to laymen. All of these words, he assured me, with confidence in his voice that I would accept everything he said as coming from God, all of them and every single one were inspired. The many sayings of Jesus that had not been recorded by St. John had been handed on from generation to generation, without losing or adding a word, until the Fathers wrote them down for us.

He recognized the incredulity in my face, for I made no attempt to hide it. And still the possibility did not occur to him that I might have a different, more creative, concept of the contribution of the Fathers to the growth of the church. There could be only one reason why I failed to acquiesce. "Do you find it difficult to understand what I am saying," he asked. Not *difficult to accept,* but *difficult to understand.* I am sure he had no inkling of his intellectual snobbery.

As we paced back and forward on top of the 20-foot-deep graves, engaged in this incredible conversation, I was recollecting a comment made the previous day at an outdoor café down the street by another priest who has long observed the Vatican scene. "The bishops are talking openly in the Synod, in the Pope's presence," he said. "He is listening and he is impressed. But don't forget that soon they depart and he stays. What is important is not what he hears in the morning in the Hall of the Broken Heads, but what he hears last thing at night, every night in his life as he goes to bed. 'Santo Padre,' says the self-assured and reassuring voice, 'do not be alarmed. The barbarians have always been at the gates, just as they are now. But providence has always picked the right man to deal with them and to defeat them. Fifteen hundred years ago, Pope Leo I met Attila, talked to him, got the better of him. Today we are equally blessed, Santo Padre. You have the blood of Leo in your veins.' "

It is in this framework that the Suenens program must be seen. There is no realistic hope for self-initiated change, certainly not at a minimally acceptable rate, because there is no awareness of need. No matter how good the people who are drawn into the system, their options are immediately reduced to what it permits. The most dangerous illusion at this time is to think that a change of persons will resolve anything. There must be a change of institutions. Structures based on the concepts and practices of medieval autocracy must be replaced, and the only model existentially available to us for the replacements is that of contemporary democracy. For an incarnational religion, that ought not to be a problem.

A Brief Biography of Paul VI

Francis X.. Murphy

Father Murphy is a professor of patristic moral
theology at the Academia Alfonsiana in Rome.
During the Second Vatican Council, he served as
a *peritus* or theological expert.
He has authored many books—among them
Politics and the Early Christian, and *Synod '67:
A New Sound in Rome,* which he coauthored
with Gary MacEoin.
Father Murphy has lectured on the Council
throughout the world. When he is in the United
States, he is a frequent radio and television guest.

The accession of Giovanni Battista Montini to the papacy is a clear indication of the fact that, for all the pretensions of its monarchically-minded jurists, the Catholic Church is actually a democratically structured organization. It is, professedly, an assembly of the people of God. Not unlike the rise of John Kennedy to the presidency of the United States, propelled by the so-called Boston Irish, Paul's path to the papacy was prepared by the enmeshment of his father and family in the church's political battles in the north of Italy, for close to half a century.

The comparison limps in the sense that Montini's father had no such obvious ambitions for his son as did Kennedy's and made no conscious political contributions in that direction. However, the historical processes involved are strikingly similar.

The election of a pope actually follows the *original* American ideal of selection by a college of his peers, the better informed representatives of the people. While the church stoutly maintains that the papal power is conferred immediately by Christ on his vicar, as head of his mystical, but visible body, the path to the papacy follows an ecclesiastical structure that is nothing if not political. The incidental historical accidents whereby a Kennedy or a Montini were positioned by the course of their individual careers, to be in line for the highest office in the state, or in the church, can be considered the workings of fate, ambition, or of divine providence. The fact is that two highly intelligent, excellently educated men of well-to-do families, with no previous lien on their respective governments by birth, became respectively president and pope.

Giovanni Battista Montini was born at 10 p.m. on September 26, 1897, in his family's villa at Concesio, a tiny suburb six miles outside of Brescia in Italy. He was the second son born to Giorgio and Giudetta Montini. His brother Ludovico had preceded him by eighteen months. Three years later, the Montinis had a third son, Francesco.

The father, Giorgio, was managing editor of the militantly Catholic daily, *Il Cittadino* of Brescia, and had financial interests in land, banking, and local political and publishing ventures. In these enterprises, he attempted to project the Catholic Church's social teachings as enunicated in Pope Leo XIII's encyclical, *Rerum Novarum* (1891), and as promoted by the speeches and writings of G. Toniolo and other Catholic sociologists. He lived in a time when the pope prohibited practicing Catholics from participating in the Italian government, a tactic that merely resulted in the country's control by anti-clericals, socialists, and radicals inimical to the church's interest.

Giorgio Montini was one of the capable men who involved themselves in the resultant civil problems, helped organize Catholic Congresses to rally their coreligionists to the cause of justice and decency, and who was finally rewarded under Pope Benedict XV with the presidency of the Catholic Electoral Union. He was one of the first Catholics permitted by the Holy See to run for public office, and was elected to parliament in the legislatures of 1919, 1922, and 1924. His career ended when, as a member of the Aventine group who boycotted the Mussolini-dominated chamber of deputies, after the political murder of the opposition candidate, Matteoti, he and his companions were physically maltreated by the Fascist terrorists.

His wife, Giudetta Montini, was of the well-to-do Alghisi family with considerable property holdings in nearby Verolavacchia and Bovezzo, where the Montini's spent a considerable part of each summer. Orphaned at the age of four, she had received an excellent convent education. Petite, good-looking, and pious, she had frail health and was introspective. She had met her husband in Rome, and despite family opposition, had married him. Her time was spent mainly in charitable activities proper to a woman of her class, and in a round of social chores incidental to the family's religious connections, and her husband's business activities. Giorgio's widowed mother, Francesca, and his sister, Maria, also lived with the family and both had considerable influence on the boys' religious development.

In keeping with the pediatric practice of the time, the new baby was put in the care of a stout peasant wet nurse on the family property near Bovezzo for his first sixteen months, on the theory that the country air and the proven health of this farmer's wife were the proper conditions for the child's immediate growth and welfare. When the baby was finally brought into the family home in Brescia, he proved frail, and for a time the wet nurse plus her own smaller children had to be lodged in town to be near the Montini household.

With his brother Ludovico, Giovanni entered school at the age of six. His primary and secondary education was under the Jesuits in their college of Cesare Arici, a private institution in whose legal rights and financial support his father Giorgio had taken great interest. The anti-clerical local government, under the Zanardelli socialists, made frequent attempts to hamper or close this institute, charging it ran counter to the state's right to control the education of its youth.

The battle over the school's survival became one of Montini's first introductions to the struggles for the rights of Catholics that would occupy most of his adult years.

To make up the time lost in class, particularly in his secondary years, he frequently had the help of a tutor. Yet, despite his health, he was an excellent student.

He also came under the influence of the Fathers of the Oratory, who conducted the nearby parish of St. John. One in particular was a young priest, Giulio Bevilaqua, who, during the tougher years of the Fascist rule, after he had publicly denounced one of Mussolini's lieutenants from the altar, had had to seek refuge in Monsignor Montini's house in Rome, remaining there on and off for five years. Bevilaqua helped Montini to enlarge his intellectual and spiritual horizons. Young "G.B.," as Montini was called by his companions, assisted with the catechetical instruction of poor children gathered in the Oratory, and frequently tutored less talented students.

Father Bevilaqua became a life-long confidant of Giovanni Montini, providing a sounding board of humor and solid common sense as counterpoints to the serious young man's intense reflection, in every stage of his career, including his first years as pope. In 1965, though Bevilaqua's days were obviously numbered, Pope Paul made him a cardinal, overcoming his objections with the self-same kind of counsels that Bevilaqua had given to Montini as a youth. He let the old cardinal return to the poor parish of which he was pastor in Brescia, where he died the following summer.

Among Giovanni Montini's first disappointments was his failure to pass the physical examination when his class was called to military service, thereby seeing his brothers and

friends march off to World War I. But he was involved in the ci-
vilian assistance programs provided for the military and particularly for the wounded.

In this period, he continued his studies. Eventually,
he decided he wanted to be a priest. His health again was at
issue and it prevented him from entering the seminary. But
through the influence of the seminary rector, a family friend,
he was allowed to take the courses as a day student. He was
ordained by the local bishop, Giacinto Gaggia, in the cathedral of Brescia, on May 29, 1920. Before going to Rome to
continue his studies, he obtained a degree in canon law on
the strength of a written paper and an examination in the Law
Faculty of the seminary in Milan.

In Rome, he lived in the Lombard college near the
Farnese Palace, and registered both in the Gregorian Univer-
sity for philosophy, and in the state University of Rome for
Letters. Within a year, however, at the insistence of Monsignor
Giuseppe Pizzardo, on the recognition of the fact that his fa-
ther was a member of parliament, he was transferred to the
Ecclesiastical College of Nobles to prepare for a career in the
church's diplomatic and administrative service.

In 1923, he spent several months as an apprentice
diplomat in the apostolic delegation in Warsaw, but the climate
proved too harsh, and he returned to Rome.

Meanwhile, however, he had made many friends
among the young Catholic university students and began to
serve as their counsellor. In particular, he had met Igino
Righetti, who had become the leader of the FUCINI, or Federation of Italian Catholic University Students. Eventually,
through the patronage of Monsignor Pizzardo, Montini was
given the official title of ecclesiastical assistant to this student
group. He collaborated with Monsignor Amleto Cicognani
who was the actual chaplain to the students at the Sapienza,
the old seat of the University of Rome. Through Cicognani he
met many prominent ecclesiastics who visited Rome.

Don G.B.M. (as the students called him) gave conferences, encouraged the founding of student papers such as the *Sapienza,* and *Azione Fucina,* for which he wrote a large number of small articles and reviews between 1924 and 1933, and quickly got involved in the politics of student life. He had to fortify and protect the students against the onslaughts of the Fascist youth organizations.

Each year, the Catholic students held a national congress, surrounding their activities with goliardic antics proper to their age. In early September, 1925, they met in Bologna, but due to the indiscretion of one of their leaders, a telegram of congratulations was sent to the king that gravely offended the pope. When they returned to Rome for the papal audience that usually topped off these gatherings, Pope Pius XI refused to see them. Montini had to break the sad news to the group who had actually risked both bodily harm and their careers in their demonstrations of defiance of the Fascist movement.

It was shortly thereafter that Montini was appointed ecclesiastical assistant of FUCINI, with Igino Righetti as president. In 1926, the National Congress was scheduled for Macerata but when the Catholic students and Montini arrived in that city, they were accosted by the police, and then set upon by Mussolini ruffians.

Montini and the leadership quickly decided to transfer to Assisi. From then on, he was engaged in a struggle to strengthen the determination of the Italian Catholic students to resist oppression without resorting to violence, but at the same time, not ceding in the least to the threats of their politically powerful opponents.

He also organized work projects for helping the poor, gave an annual series of conferences on the Christian way of life, the faith, and Catholic doctrine, which were later published as books. He introduced the students to the liturgy in monthly days of retreat at the Benedictine abbey attached to the Basilica of St. Paul.

He took part in the discussion that led to the founding of a similar federation for Catholic University graduates, for whom he translated Maritain's *The Three Reformers,* and Grandmaison's *A Personal Religion.* He helped organize the Catholic publishing house Studium, and advised the Morcelliana press of Brescia in their selection of foreign books dealing with Catholic intellectual interests. He had spent the summer of 1924 in Paris, mastering both the French language and literature. He studied German with the aid of Dom Winzen, an American Benedictine, and worked hard at learning English so he could read Shakespeare and the English novelists.

By 1933, the pressure of his work in the Vatican Secretariat of State became all absorbing, and Monsignor Pizzardo suggested to Pius XI that Montini be relieved of outside tasks. He continued, however, to give courses in diplomatic history at the College of Nobles until 1937 when, in December, he was named Substitute Secretary of State for Ordinary Affairs.

By his side, Monsignor Domenico Tardini was selected as the Substitute Secretary for Extraordinary Affairs, mostly the diplomatic relations of the Holy See. The two prelates, though totally different in character and interest, became a team. They worked together first under Cardinal Eugenio Pacelli until he became Pope Pius XII in 1939, and under Cardinal Maglione until his death in 1944. Pius XII then decided not to appoint a new Cardinal Secretary of State, and the full burden fell upon his two substitute secretaries.

But the pope was also using Montini as his personal assistant, confiding to his care many other difficult projects such as the organization of the Vatican's Information Service for the tracing of missing persons, refugees, and prisoners of war on both sides involved in World War II. He was given control of the efforts made by the pope in the relief of the starving and homeless in many parts of the world, from North Africa to India and China, and of the Vatican's contributions to rebuilding Europe as well as Italy in the postwar years.

He likewise had to supervise Vatican efforts for the resettlement of the millions of refugees and displaced persons who swarmed into Western Germany, Austria, Italy, and France upon the cessation of hostilities. The U. S. Catholic War Relief Services then became one of his major collaborators, as it grappled with the relief and refugee problems in all the war afflicted areas of the world. He used its officials in the numerous contacts the Holy See made with both governments and voluntary agencies, and more particularly in direct and indirect dealings with UNRRA, the International Refuge Organization, and the numerous activities of the United Nations that were pursued in the postwar period.

It was the papal nuncio in Paris, Archbishop Angelo Roncalli who had insisted that the Holy See recognize and collaborate with UNESCO, and Montini immediately saw the wisdom of the nuncio's suggestion. Over great curial opposition, he pushed the project through. In Italy, he arranged for the organization of the Pontifical Works of Assistance that, in its early years, fed and clothed the homeless and displaced with the material and monetary aid it received from War Relief Services.

In May, 1938, Montini had accompanied Cardinal Pacelli, the papal legate, to the Eucharistic Congress in Budapest. The war and its aftermath prevented further travel. But in the summer of 1951, he accepted invitations to make a flying visit to the United States. There, he visited most of the larger dioceses, received a degree from Notre Dame University, *honoris causa,* along with President Dwight Eisenhower, and wound up in Quebec. He was welcomed by the many friends he had made through his activities in the Vatican, particularly during the war, and in his work during the post-war rebuilding.

Then, in 1960, he made another visit to the United States and Brazil.

In 1962, he undertook a similar trip through most

of Africa, south of the Sahara. He was then the Cardinal of Milan, and it was not without the encouragement—if not the suggestion—of Pope John that he had undertaken such rapid and strenuous trips. They served, however, as a harbinger for his voyages as pope from Jerusalem to Constantinople, and New York, and then half way round the world, to India and Colombia.

Meanwhile, in the Italian election campaign of 1948, the pope and the Holy See made no secret of their total and vigorous support for the Christian Democratic party headed by Alcide de Gaspari. And Montini had a good deal to do with the technical side of the Vatican activities.

By 1954, however, there were two decidedly divergent viewpoints regarding the continuance of this interference in Italian political affairs. Under Dr. Luigi Gedda, the lay leader of Catholic Action, and a majority of the members of the Curia, strong, open political participation was favored as the only valid means of containing the influence of the Communist and Radical parties—particularly among the workers.

On the other hand, both the prime minister, Alcide de Gaspari, and Don Luigi Sturzo, the founder of the Italian Popular party before World War I, who had returned to Italy after a long exile, were convinced that the Italian political situation would never stabilize until the Vatican receded completely from interference. Montini supported the de Gaspari-Sturzo cause.

When the Christian Democrats lost a series of local elections, the strong curial party known as the "pentagon," under the guidance of Cardinals Pizzardo and Micara, and Monsignors Tardini, Ottaviani, and Ruffini, decided that Montini had to go. They brought pressure on Pope Pius XII who was chronically sick at the time. When Cardinal Schuster of Milan died in November, 1954, they seized their opportunity.

They insisted that Montini be selected as the new archbishop of this great Catholic metropolis, torn by factions and all but dominated by Communist labor leaders. It would be a realistic test of both his abilities and his political theories.

Pius XII finally gave in. But the day of Montini's consecration, December 12, 1954, the pope was confined to his bed. Nevertheless, over the radio, he broadcast a tribute to the new archbishop. On arriving in Milan, Archbishop Montini kissed the soil on the city's outskirts, and announced to the poor and laboring classes that he was their pastor, interested and concerned about all their problems. During the next seven years, he exhausted himself in proving his sincerity by visiting, counseling, and assisting everyone with whom he could come into contact. He said mass in foundries and industrial plants, attended sport and festival activities, gave conferences and preached on every possible occasion. In 1955, he organized a vast, diocesan-wide parish mission, only to discover that this type of evangelization, though meticulously advertised and prepared, was a thing of the past.

Upon his arrival in Milan, he was visited by the patriarch of Venice, Cardinal Angelo Roncalli, who reassured him that his obvious banishment from the Vatican was no great tragedy. In the course of his career, Roncalli had also fallen from curial grace, and yet survived.

Then when Roncalli became Pope John XXIII, Archbishop Montini headed John's list as the first of the cardinals he created. As John's vision of the Council matured, he found himself relying more and more on the cardinal of Milan for support and advice. When the Council opened, John invited him to take up quarters in the Vatican, the only conciliar prelate from the outside to receive this courtesy.

Montini only spoke twice during the first session, at the beginning and toward the close. It seemed as though he had been requested by John to hold his fire. But he had written a series of letters for publication in the Milan Catholic weekly in which he strongly criticized the repressive attitude of the conservative group, particularly among the Curia. This frank attitude apparently dispelled Pope John's concern about

Montini's strength of commitment, and his ability to make tough decisions.

When Montini seconded the proposal of the Belgian Cardinal Suenens who had John's full support for his contention that the Council should straighten out its lines of development by devoting its attention to the church *ad intra,* its internal structure and meaning, and the church *ad extra,* its dealing with the contemporary world, the die was cast. John selected him as the man he would most like to have succeed him.

The dying pontiff made no sign as to his preference; but it was not difficult for the majority of cardinals, who favored John's policy of opening the windows of the church, to see whom he thought best fitted to carry on the revolutionary enterprise John had inaugurated.

On June 21, 1963, the College of Cardinals on its fifth ballot elected Giovanni Battista Montini as Pope Paul VI.

Chronology
of Paul VI's Reign

James F. Andrews

Although every attempt has been made to make the following chronology complete in the essential dates of Paul's reign, it is, of course, far from exhaustive.

In addition to the historic dates of the reign, others are included because they are interesting or particularly significant.

No attempt has been made to chronicle the documents or the debate at the Second Vatican Council. This has been done elsewhere. Our chief purpose here was to provide a handy guide to the reader who may want to see the relationship of various statements or actions of the pontificate to date.

The chief sources of factual data were: the *National Catholic Reporter*, *The Pope Speaks*, and *The New York Times*. The editor accepts responsibility for error; when variant dates were available, the date on the document referred to was accepted rather than its public release date.

June 21, 1963   The College of Cardinals elected Cardinal Giovanni Battista Montini as the 261st Supreme Pontiff of the

Universal Church. He chose the name Pope Paul VI.

June 30, 1963
Coronation ceremonies were held in St. Peter's Square. The title of the coronation homily was "The Voice of the Modern World."

September 21, 1963
Pope Paul announced his intent to reform the Roman Curia. The reform to include a clear definition of jurisdiction of each office or congregation, the unclogging of communications among these offices and between them and the pope. The reform would also seek to guarantee the rights of the individual before the massive bureaucracy of the Curia. The pope also mentioned the creation of new offices and the internationalization of the Curia personnel.

September 29, 1963
The second session of the Council opened. The session ended December 4, 1963.

January 4, 1964
Pope Paul boarded a jet plane for a flight to Amman, capital city of Jordan, and the starting point of his unprecedented journey to the Holy Land. While in Jerusalem, the pope had two cordial meetings with Patriarch Athenagoras, leader of 150 million Orthodox Christians. The meetings represented the first contact between the leaders of the two churches since 1439. He returned to Rome from Israel on January 5.

May 17, 1964   Paul announced the formation of a
                          new Vatican Secretariat for Relations
                          with non-Christian Religions.

June 23, 1964   Pope Paul, in a speech assessing the
                          first year of his pontificate and dis-
                          cussing the tasks of the next year, re-
                          iterated Pope Pius XII's norms on
                          birth control.

August 6, 1964   In the second year of his pontificate,
                          Pope Paul issued his first encyclical
                          letter, *Ecclesiam Suam*. It was a pol-
                          icy paper in which he described the
                          tasks confronting the church, and es-
                          pecially the church in Council.

September 14, 1964   The third session of the Vatican
                          Council was opened.

November 21, 1964   The third session of the Council
                          closed. It was at this session that Paul
                          declared Mary to be Mother of the
                          church.

December 2–5, 1964   Pope Paul flew 4,000 miles to India
                          for the 38th International Eucharistic
                          Congress in Bombay. He was there
                          for four days. While in India, the pope
                          made an appeal for all nations to di-
                          vert "even part of the expenditure on
                          arms to the relief of the many prob-
                          lems of nutrition, clothing, shelter,
                          and medical care which affect so
                          many peoples."

April 29, 1965   In the second year of his pontificate,
                          Paul issued his second encyclical,
                          Mense Maio. It was a brief but vigor-

ous appeal for prayers to beg Mary's intercession for peace and for the success of the Council.

August 8, 1965 The pope recalled the 20th Anniversary of Hiroshima and called it an "infernal slaughter."

September 3, 1965 In the third year of his pontificate, Paul released an encyclical entitled *Mysterium Fidei*. It was on the doctrine and worship of the Holy Eucharist. A conservative document, it was widely discussed because of its release just before the beginning of the fourth session of the Council.

September 14, 1965 The pope announced the establishment of the Synod of Bishops on the opening day of the Ecumenical Council's last session. He followed it up the next day with a document spelling out how Synod's members will be chosen and outlining the rules which govern it.

October 4, 1965 Pope Paul flew to New York City to address the United Nations General Assembly. It was the 20th Anniversary of the United Nations. In this address he made the famous plea: "Never again war, never again."

His exhausting schedule included an open air Mass in Yankee Stadium and a visit to the Vatican Pavilion at the World's Fair. He returned to Rome the same evening and went

directly to the Council upon his return October 5th to report to the
Council fathers on his trip.

October 11, 1965   Pope Paul sent a letter to the Second
Vatican Council in which he re-
moved the topic of celibacy from the
Council's competence.

December 4, 1965   Pope Paul joined in an unprecedented formal service invoking Chris-
tian unity with 65 delegate-observers
of non-Catholic churches to the Ecumenical Council. They met with
Pope Paul and nearly 1,000 cardinals
and bishops for the service in St.
Paul's Outside-the-Walls. He said, "A
great stretch of the road remains to
be brought behind us, but we have
begun to love one another." His
voice almost trembling with emo-
tion: "Your departure with the end of
the Council leaves in us a loneliness
which before the Council we did not
know, and which now makes us feel
sad. We would like to have you with
us always!"

After the service, Dr. Albert Outler,
Methodist observer at the Council,
called it "one of the three or four
most significant moments of the entire Council."

December 7, 1965   The pope issued an apostolic letter
changing the name and the regula-
tions of the Sacred Congregation of
the Holy Office. The new name: The

Congregation for the Doctrine of the Faith.

December 7, 1965   Pope Paul VI and Athenagoras I, with his Holy Synod, jointly lifted Catholic-Orthodox excommunication.

December 8, 1965   The fourth and final session of the Second Vatican Council ended.

December 22, 1965   Pope Paul issued a Christmas address in which he called for an end to racism and nationalism and urged disarmament.

February 17, 1966   In a document called *Paenitemini*, Pope Paul made extensive changes in church regulations on penance.

March 23, 1966   Pope Paul met with Anglican primate Michael Ramsey, the archbishop of Canterbury, for two days of meetings. At the end of their cordial meetings, they issued a joint statement in which they pledged to begin a "serious dialogue" which may lead to unity. Their meetings ended in a prayer service at St. Paul's Outside-the-Walls. Archbishop Ramsey admitted that mixed marriages remain a problem.

March 26, 1966   In the fourth year of his pontificate, Pope Paul issued *Populorum Progressio*. He called this, his fifth encyclical, "a vast program of action on behalf of developing nations" seeking to assure "economic suffi-

ciency, moral dignity, and worldwide cooperation."

April 27, 1966

Pope Paul met with Soviet Foreign
Minister Andrei Gromyko for 40
minutes in the pontiff's private library. It was the first time in history
a pope has received a foreign minister of a Communist nation at the
Vatican.

May 13, 1966

Pope Paul flew to Portugal to pray
for peace in the church and in the
world in the Shrine of Our Lady of
Fatima. He returned to Rome the
same day. The occasion for the
pope's visit was the celebration of the
50th anniversary of the apparition of
the Blessed Virgin to the Children at
Fatima and the 25th anniversary of
the consecration of the world to the
Immaculate Heart of Mary by Pope
Pius XII.

June 28, 1966

A commission of specialists, the international papal birth control commission, gave its report to the pope.

August 12, 1966

Pope Paul issued interpretations of
Second Vatican Council decrees on
bishops, priests, religious orders, and
missions that tended toward the de-
centralization of authority and the
sharing of church rule by Rome with
the hierarchy around the world. The
document was called *Ecclesiae Sanc-
tae*. In it he urged bishops and priests
to ask for retirement before the age

of 75. It was later confirmed by the Vatican that the retirement age did not apply to prelates in the Roman Curia.

September 15, 1966   Pope Paul issued the encyclical *Christi Matri*. He urged negotiation upon world leaders. He called on Catholics to pray the Rosary during October for true peace and for the removal of attitudes which tend to foster war.

October 29, 1966   Speaking before the national congress of the Italian Society of Obstetricians and Gynecologists, the pope said that he would delay his decision on birth control "for some time yet."

Speaking of the international commission which presented a report to him of 800 pages on June 28, 1966, he said, "It seems to us, nevertheless, that these conclusions cannot be considered definitive, because of the fact that they carry grave implications together with several other weighty questions both in the sphere of doctrine and in the pastoral and social spheres which cannot be isolated or set aside, but which demand a logical consideration in the context of what precisely is under study."

The pope said: "We know that people are waiting for us to give a decisive pronouncement regarding the thought of the church on this question. But obviously we cannot make such a pronouncement in this particular instance."

He said: "The norm until now taught by the church cannot be considered not binding, as if the magisterium (or teaching authority) of the church were in a state of doubt at the present time."

May 16, 1967

Pope Paul asked for a lowering of the barriers to religious freedom in China and said that he would like to discuss peace with Chinese leaders.

May 24, 1967

Pope Paul pleaded with the United States to stop bombing North Vietnam and he asked North Vietnam to halt infiltration of arms and war materials into the South. "It is . . . . necessary that bombing over the territory of the North should cease, and it is necessary that at the same time the infiltration of arms and war materials into the South should cease." "It is also necessary that all acts of terrorism, which do not contribute either to the honor of the good and hard-working people of Vietnam, or to the concord and peace which is so much desired, should cease.   In a word: Every form of violence must cease!"

June 23, 1967

Paul released an encyclical called *Sacerdotalis Caelibatus*, which clearly restated the church's insistence on celibacy for priests of the Latin rite.

June 27, 1967

The pope restored the permanent diaconate.

June 29, 1967

The "Year of Faith" began. It coincided with the nineteenth centenary observance of the martyrdom of Saints Peter and Paul. Pope Paul called for the "Year of Faith" because: "Today doubts are raised about everything in the world of thought, and therefore that of religion. It seems as if the mind of modern man finds no rest except in total negation, the abandonment of any servitude, of any faith."

The "Year of Faith" was proclaimed in an apostolic exhortation entitled *Petrum et Paulum Apostolos* published February 22, 1967 in the *L'Osservatore Romano*.

July 25, 1967

Pope Paul flew to Istanbul to pray for unity between the Roman and the Orthodox Churches and to seek peace in the Middle East. It was the first visit by a Roman pope to historic Constantinople in 1,000 years. It was also the first time a reigning pope had prayed in an Orthodox church. While in Turkey, the pope met with Athenagoras, the Orthodox patriarch—their second meeting. He also met with leaders of the Turkish government.

This was the pope's fifth trip abroad. It lasted two days.

August 15, 1967

The pope issued the document reforming and reorganizing the Roman Curia. The reform went into effect March 1, 1968.

September 22, 1967

Pope Paul sent a letter to United Nations Secretary General U Thant, praising new initiatives in peace-making, "underway or planned," and offering his help to the international body in any way it might consider useful."

September 29, 1967

The first worldwide Synod of Bishops was convened in Rome. The solemn closing took place on October 29, 1967.

October 11, 1967

The World Congress of the Lay Apostolate met in Rome from October 11 to the 19th.

October 26, 1967

Pope Paul met with Ecumenical Orthodox Patriarch Athenagoras in St. Peter's Basilica. They ended their meetings on October 28, 1967 by calling for greater efforts toward world peace and Christian unity. They had three meetings at the Vatican.

January 1, 1968

A day proclaimed by Pope Paul as World Peace Day. In his talk, the pope referred to "the tremendous disaster of a spreading war, a needless war," and said that "new, terrible obstacles" are arising to complicate the pursuit of peace. He spoke about Vietnam and seemed to be critical of the policy of "hot pursuit" which was being considered by the Johnson administration, a policy which would send U. S. troops into Cambodia where the Communists have been reported to have established bases. He called for a truce in Vietnam.

March 1, 1968

Reorganization of the Roman Curia went into effect. It put the Secretariat of State in charge of coordinating all the Curia's work. The office of the Secretary of State has thereby acquired major weight because the Secretary will preside at meetings of all heads of congregations.

Under the new terms of the reform, the former lifetime appointments of heads of congregations have been rescinded. They are now five-year appointments, renewable at the pleasure of the pope, and all appointments officially end at the death of the pope.

June 30, 1968

Pope Paul, at the closing of the "Year of Faith" during an open air mass in St. Peter's Square, proclaimed a 3,000-word *Credo of the People of God*. He described it as a "profession of faith." "We shall accordingly make a profession of faith, pronounce a creed which, without being strictly speaking, a dogmatic definition, repeats in substance, some development called for by the spiritual condition of our time, the creed of Nicaea, the creed of the immortal tradition of the holy church of God." The occasion for the *Credo* was what he described as "the disquiet which agitates certain modern quarters with regard to the faith. They do not escape the influence of the world being profoundly changed, in which so many certainties are being disputed or discussed. We see even Catholics allowing themselves to be seized by a kind of passion for change and novelty."

The pope's *Credo* was issued five days before the opening of the fourth assembly of the World Council of Churches at Uppsala. Dr. Eugene Carson Blake, head of the World Council, referred to the *Credo* as "a conservative statement." Dr. Lukas Vischer, secretary of the Department of Faith and Order, said the timing of the *Credo* was "unfortunate."

The World Council meeting is held every seven years; representatives from 232 denominations attended this one.

July 29, 1968

Humanae Vitae, Pope Paul's long-awaited encyclical on birth control was issued. It was dated four days before it was released.

One of the results of the post-*Humanae Vitae* period was an intense discussion of papal authority. Various national conferences of bishops, issued statements which seemed to interpret the encyclical's ban on birth control in less absolute terms. For example, the statements of the French, German, Belgian, and Canadian hierarchies. Subsequently, the practical question of the pope consulting more collegially with the world's bishops before pronouncing on matters of interest to the universal church became a key point for the forthcoming Synod of Bishops.

The encyclical insisted on the norm of natural law that "each and every act must remain open to the transmission of life." It triggered worldwide reaction—with notable protest and dissent in many parts of the world.

July 31, 1968

Speaking of how he formed his decision on birth control, the pope said, "How often we have the impression of being almost overwhelmed by this mass of documentation and how often, humanly speaking, we have felt the inadequacy of our humble person for the formidable apostolic obligation of having to pronounce on the matter."

August 22, 1968

The pope took the sixth air journey of his reign, this time to Bogotá, Colombia, for the 39th International Eucharistic Congress. He also presided at the opening of the Latin American Bishops' Conference. On August 23 the pope spent the day in the slums of Bogotá.

December 25, 1968   Pope Paul celebrated midnight Mass in Taranto, the modern center of the Italian steel industry.

March 26, 1969   Pope Paul created a one million dollar fund to foster the development of Latin America. The initial one million dollars will be devoted to farm workers of Colombia for agrarian reform. The aid will take the form of interest free loans for up to 50 years. The Inter-American Development Bank in Washington, D. C. will have the responsibility for determining the loan projects, in consultation with the Holy See.

April 28, 1969   The International Theological Commission called for by the first Synod of Bishops was formed by Pope Paul at a secret consistory of the cardinals. He named 30 world renowned theologians to the Commission three days later.

May 15, 1969   Pope Paul sent Cardinal Patrick O'Boyle, archbishop of Washington, D. C., a letter supporting the Cardinal in his conflict with his dissenting priests over the birth control encyclical. It is the only known case of the pope's public support on a local level since the encyclical was issued.

May 28, 1969

Cardinal Leo Suenens crystallized debate on papal authority prior to the second Synod of Bishops by granting an extensive interview which was published simultaneously in several languages. The interview on "collegiality" and "coresponsibility" was published in the United States by the *National Catholic Reporter.* Reply was immediately forthcoming from the Vatican. The dean of the College of Cardinals, Cardinal Eugene Tisserant, criticized Suenens for the interview. Others soon joined in the debate, notably Cardinal Jean Daniélou.

June 10, 1969

Pope Paul visited the headquarters of the World Council of Churches in Geneva. In an address at the Council's headquarters he said that membership of the Roman Catholic Church in the World Council was "still too soon." The main occasion for his trip to Geneva was to visit the headquarters of the International Labor Organization, marking its 50th anniversary.

July 31, 1969

Pope Paul made a historic trip to Uganda, Africa, the first pope in history to set foot in Africa. It was a three-day visit. While in Uganda he met with the Biafran and Nigerian government representatives to attempt to bring about negotiations. On August 3, 1969, when he had returned from Africa, he did an African dance at his weekly general audience to show how the African nuns had danced for him.

October 6, 1969   The pope opened the three-day session of the newly formed International Theological Commission in Rome.

October 11, 1969   Pope Paul opened the second Synod of Bishops. The pre-Synodal debate had raised expectations that the sessions would be stormy. However, the results were optimistic.

October 27, 1969   Pope Paul, in the last working session of the Synod of Bishops, accepted three of the bishops' proposals: to call Synods at least every two years; to expand the Secretariat of the Synod to include bishops from all over the world; and to allow the bishops to suggest themes for the agenda of further Synods. He promised to give thoughtful consideration to the other proposals of the Synod.